Out of the
DARKNESS

Out of the DARKNESS

The Untold Story of Jewish Revival in the Former Soviet Union

Sandra Teplinsky

Foreword by Jonathan Bernis

HOIM
Publishing

Hear O Israel Publishing
Jacksonville Beach, Florida

ISBN #: 0-9663844-0-7

Printed in the United States of America

Dedicated to two special Messianic Jews from Russia,
Kasenya Rebecca and Daria Batya;
to the many faithful believers
whose stories comprise this book;
and most of all,
to *Yeshua HaMashiach,* the Lord Jesus Christ

Acknowledgments

THIS BOOK COULD NEVER HAVE BECOME A REALITY without the unconditional love and support, as well as tireless technical assistance, of my husband Scott. Thank you for laying down your life for me.

Thank you to my mother, Esther Gerstein, who never gave up encouraging me to write, and who helped pray me into the kingdom of God.

Thank you to the many intercessors who prayed for years for the completion of this book, especially dear friends Romy Zarit, Nancy Lang, Cindi Fink, Sue Ekenberg, Cheri LaBaron, and Carol Howell.

Thank you to the leaders, editor, and volunteer workers with Hear O Israel Ministries, who gave of their time and efforts to provide me with stories that unfold in the following pages.

Thank you to the countless believers in the former Soviet Union who love the Lord Yeshua and hold to the Word of His testimony.

Most of all, thank you, God of Israel, for your faithfulness to your people through all generations.

Contents

Foreword

WHEN I FIRST WENT TO RUSSIA IN MAY, 1990, I had no idea what to expect. It was, more or less, a fact-finding mission to understand the condition of the Jewish people. Little did I know that, during those six short days, God would radically change the course of my life.

I can still remember my first impressions. On the one hand, I was shocked by the decay and disrepair which greeted me. Russia, the land, was a gloomy, dark, repressive and poverty stricken place. Its people, however, were another matter. From almost the moment I arrived, I was heartily embraced by some of the warmest, most open and hospitable people I had ever known. They were eager for interaction with Westerners, searching for truth, and hungry for spiritual reality. I fell in love with them almost overnight.

The team I was leading took several hundred bibles and pieces of literature with us. We wanted to distribute them all but we had no idea how to go about it. This was still the Soviet Union, for one thing. Besides, we'd only be in St. Petersburg (then called Leningrad) and Moscow a few days.

What happened next amazed us all. No sooner had we given a piece of literature to someone on the street than we became swamped with Russians, all clamoring for whatever Gospel materials we had. Within minutes, every bit of literature was gone!

Even more amazing, it seemed as if almost every person we met was Jewish. Were there just a lot of Jewish people in Moscow and St. Petersburg, I wondered, or were we witnessing the divine orchestration of the Holy Spirit? I could feel my spirit racing. I knew I was in the middle of something *miraculous*. I had to return.

Over the next two years, I led several more teams to the Soviet Union. This time, we not only gave out literature, but we discipled new believers and, eventually, helped some of them establish a Messianic congregation in Minsk, Belarus. My burden for these people was growing; still, I relegated my service there to "supplementary missions trip" status. As the leader of a successful Messianic congregation, my life was cozy and secure and my ministry was thriving.

Then it happened. I was flying home from Moscow when the Spirit of God began dealing with me about making a more serious commitment to Russia — one that would ultimately result in laying down my life and my congregation.

By that time, the Iron Curtain had come down. Thousands of missionaries had poured into the former Soviet Union. Only a handful of them, however, were reaching out to the millions of Jews in the land.

I knew God wanted to reach this remnant with the Good News — before they returned to the Promised Land. I also knew He was calling me to play a more significant role in the reaping. I didn't understand how I was to do this. I only felt Him drawing me to return to St. Petersburg. I knew it was an invitation, not a command, yet I understood it to be God's perfect will for my life.

I hadn't been to St. Petersburg since that first visit two years ago. Yet the leading of God was unmistakable. Several months later, only out of obedience, I returned. It was then that the idea for Messianic Jewish music festivals was born. I knew the Jewish people of Russia were greatly interested in Israel and Jewish culture. I also knew that Russian people in general had a great love for music and the arts. Organizing a festival of Jewish music and dance seemed to offer the perfect platform for sharing the Good News in a Jewish way with the Russian people.

After a lot of groping about, discovering how to organize such an event in a country that had no rhyme or reason, our first festival took place May 12–16, 1993, at the Oktobersky Concert Hall in St. Petersburg. Over 85 Americans, Israelis and Europeans joined us, serving as volunteer staff.

We had no idea what the results would be or how many people would come. So we were all shocked on opening night to find the 4000-seat hall filled to overflowing. Even more stunning, following a short message and altar call, over 50 percent of the crowd — half of them Jewish — eagerly rushed to the front of the concert hall to pray.

Many on the team began to weep as they experienced something which, to the best of my knowledge, had not happened in almost 2000 years.

Over the next four years, we saw thousands more Jewish people respond to altar calls and receive physical healings, and were able to minister the love of God on city streets, in hospitals, orphanages and other public facilities. God was using the hundreds of volunteer staffers that, by now, were joining us for the festivals — and revolutionizing their own lives as He had mine several years before.

Also, by the grace of God, a dozen new Messianic congregations were launched or strengthened by the festivals. Messianic congregations are now thriving in St. Petersburg and Moscow, Russia; Kiev, Odessa, Zhitomir, Zaporoshye, Dnepropetrovsk, Chernovtsi and Nikolaev, Ukraine; Minsk, Belarus; Riga, Latvia; and Kishinev, Moldova. Many others have been spawned indirectly.

Fourteen separate Messianic Jewish Music Festivals have been held by Hear O Israel Ministries since its inception in 1993. As of 1998, more than 300,000 people in the former Soviet Union had been reached through the festivals. The largest, drawing over 60,000 people, was held at the central football stadium in Odessa, Ukraine, in 1995. Through the mercy of God, over 150,000 people, 75,000 of them Jewish, have responded to altar calls at the festivals. God is at work among the Jewish people in a way that we have not witnessed since the first century.

A Messianic Jewish bible school, co-sponsored by Hear O Israel and several other Christian and Messianic Jewish organizations, now operates in Odessa, Ukraine, as well. Messianic believers from all over the former Soviet Union train there for ministry.

As I've observed this phenomenon, the miracle — as I see it — is not so much that the Jewish people are deeply hungry for the Gospel or spiritual things (although many are) but that they don't have the same bias against the Gospel that you find among Jewish people in the West. Jewish people in America and Europe often grow up inculturated against the Gospel. Because of 2000 years of anti-Semitism and a false presentation of true Christianity, the standard position of American and Western European Jews towards the Gospel is often, "Oh, I'm Jewish," as if to say "I'm excluded" or "I'm exempt" from the Gospel message. The average Jew living in the West would not come to a festival such as ours, no matter how outstanding the performers, if they knew they were going to hear about Jesus as the Messiah.

In Russia and other former Soviet republics, because of 70 years of communism, such a bias does not exist. Though we clearly communicate in all our promotional materials that attendees will hear the Gospel, people still come in droves — most notably hundreds of Holocaust survivors who have endured much suffering at the hands of so-called Christians. Although many are attracted to the offer of a free concert, many others have told me they came primarily to hear the Gospel! That Jews would turn out — *en masse* — to an event in which they knew they would hear the Gospel is phenomenal indeed; something, I believe, that only God could sovereignly plan and orchestrate.

Just a decade ago, mass outreach in Jewish ministry was unheard of. Never in our wildest dreams could we ever have imagined such a great harvest — one that not only paralleled but even eclipsed the harvest witnessed by first century believers. Yet God had promised such a day would come:

> *"'However, the days are coming,' declares the Lord, 'when men will no longer say, "As surely as the Lord lives, who brought the Israelites up out of Egypt," but they will say, "As surely as the Lord lives, who brought the Israelites up out of the land of the north and out of all the countries where He had banished them." For I will restore them to the land I gave their forefathers.'"*
>
> Jeremiah 16:14-16

The Scriptures teach clearly that there is an inseparable connection between the spiritual restoration of the Jewish people to their Messiah and their physical return to the Land of Israel (See Deuteronomy 30). The promise of physical restoration to the Land, referred to in the passage above, necessitates a concomitant spiritual awakening. What God has started in Russia and the republics of the former Soviet Union is only the beginning. The restoration of the Jewish people will ultimately be worldwide.

Sandy and Scott Teplinsky have been invaluable members of our team since shortly after our festivals began. Scott has been a driving force behind our humanitarian aid efforts. Sandy has always been hungry for a true move of God among her people. Since I've known her, her motto has always been "More, Lord!" She has been diligent to chronicle the remarkable events that have taken place through these festivals and to delve deeply into the lives of these precious people who have been changed by the power of God.

Interweaving her narrative with Biblical truths regarding God's plan for the Jewish people, she opens the reader's eyes and helps them understand, in a deeper way, the significance of this time of harvest and its implications for the body of Messiah.

The restoration of the Jewish people is one of the most significant prophetic events yet to take place before the return of Jesus to this earth. As you read this book, I think it will bring you closer to understanding the prophetic significance of what is happening in the former Soviet Union, its import to believers throughout the earth, and how it relates to Romans 11:15:

> *"For if their (the Jewish people's) rejection is the reconciliation of the world, what will their acceptance be but life from the dead."*

We are living in astounding times, when the eyes of those long blinded are being opened and those held captive are being set free. May the Holy Spirit enlighten your heart, enabling you to understand the truths contained in this book and give you a loving burden for the lost sheep of the house of Israel.

> *"For my heart's desire and prayer for Israel is that they may be saved."*   Romans 10:1

Jonathan Bernis
Executive Director
Hear O Israel Ministries

Preface

"The people walking in darkness have seen a great light; on those living in the land of the shadow of death a light has dawned."
Isaiah 9:2

". . . I will cut through bars of iron. I will give you the treasures of darkness, riches stored in secret places..."   Isaiah 45:3

DANCING AND SINGING IN THE STREETS...tambourines and flutes resounding . . . banners flying and tears flowing. Children laughing, their parents shouting, "Hosanna to our King!"

Just ten years ago, who would have fathomed this scenario taking place behind the Iron Curtain? Yet today, as thousands of Jews in cities across the former USSR embrace *Yeshua* (Hebrew for Jesus) as their Messiah, it is as if the Father in heaven has thrown an enormous party to welcome home these prodigal sons and daughters of Jacob.

Since 1993, from Moscow to Minsk, from Kiev to Kishinev, over 75,000 Jews have come out of the darkness and turned to Jesus as their personal Savior. Many of these new believers are survivors of the Nazi Holocaust. Other, younger ones, are emigrating to Israel, carrying their contagious, fiery faith with them. Still others are staying behind, forming fledgling Messianic Jewish congregations in these historically anti-Semitic lands. Not since the days recorded in the Book of Acts have so many Jews responded to the Gospel. In the dawn of Israel's Jubilee (50th anniversary) celebration in 1998, what could this phenomenon portend for that nation, the church and perhaps even the world?

From 1994 to 1996, I participated in seven short-term mission trips to the former Soviet Union with Hear O Israel Ministries, an

xvii

organization headquartered in Jacksonville Beach, Florida, dedicated to reaching Jewish people worldwide with the Good News. Serving on my first mission as a street evangelist together with my husband, I was astonished at the extraordinary and supernatural nature of what took place before my eyes, minute by minute. In two decades of Jewish ministry, I had neither seen nor heard of so many Jewish people embracing the Gospel message. I was witnessing the Lord break down gates of bronze, cut through bars of iron, and bring out of the darkness treasures and riches stored in secret places. It was a story that had to had to be told.

As an attorney, I was accustomed to recording facts and gathering evidence. I also had a heart for the people of the former Soviet Union, as all of my grandparents had come from Russia and Ukraine. Thus I became the ministry's journalist for the next three years. The result is this book, a chronicle of an unprecedented revival among God's chosen people.

All the stories, events, and narrative detail recounted herein took place as described. Most of the conversations have been repeated practically verbatim. The rest has been described as accurately as memory allows. Only a few minor details have been slightly modified—and then only to assist with the flow of the text.

Out of the Darkness is neither a history nor a theology book. However, to fully appreciate what God is doing and how that relates to the church at large, some historical and Biblical context is essential. Therefore, the story is interwoven with some discussion of historical and theological issues relevant to the church's prophetic relationship with the Jewish people.

Psalm 66:5 says, "Come and see what God has done, how awesome His works in man's behalf!" That is the invitation issued by this book. May those reading the pages that follow be inspired, encouraged and challenged in their understanding of God's heart and plan for His people in these last days.

"I say then have they [Israel] stumbled that they should fall? Certainly not! But through their fall, to provoke them to jealousy, salvation has come to the Gentiles. Now if their fall is riches for the world, and their failure riches for the Gentiles, how much more their fullness! . . . For if their being cast away is the reconciling of the world, what will their acceptance be but life from the dead?"

Romans 11:11–12, 15 (NKJ)

1

A Heritage Invaded

"But Zion said, 'The Lord has forsaken me, the Lord has forgotten me.' Can a mother forget her nursing child she has borne? Though she may forget, I will not forget you! See, I have engraved you on the palms of My hands; your walls are ever before Me."

Isaiah 49:14-16

LIKE MUCH OF THE REST OF UKRAINE, our austere hotel room in the city of Odessa is crumbling from disrepair. Chunks of floor, wall and ceiling collapse at random, creating a dusty mosaic of dangling wires and pipes. The electricity has not been turned off this evening, however. We are thankful. With it, we can use the hotel elevator, wobbly though it is, and walk about with a reasonable amount of light. Trudging up fourteen flights of stairs to our room in pitch darkness is not the reception we have in mind for our guest, a Ukrainian Jewish survivor of the Nazi Holocaust. Nearly seventy years of age, Leonid's weakened body belies a tenacious will—and mind still in full command of its encyclopedic contents. The stairs would have proved challenging to him, but nonetheless undaunting.

It is the summer of 1995 and we are in Ukraine to bring good news: Israel's Messiah has come. Leonid thinks this is news indeed. He says he is interested and wants to know more.

Leonid is one of a hundred or so Holocaust survivors in Odessa who have just heard that the God of Abraham, Isaac and Jacob loves them. At last, they have been told that in Yeshua (Hebrew for Jesus), their "hard service has been completed. . .[their] sin has been paid for, . . .that [they] have received from the Lord's hand double for all [their] sins." (Isaiah 40:2) To these who have come through fire, "who grieve in Zion," the Lord has extended "a crown of beauty instead of ashes, the oil of gladness instead of mourning and a garment of praise instead of a spirit of despair." (Isaiah 61:3)

As this second millennium draws to a close, Jews in the former Soviet Union are embracing Yeshua as their Messiah in numbers reminiscent of the New Testament Book of Acts. Since 1994, over 150,000 of these sons and daughters of Abraham, Isaac and Jacob have heard the gospel. At least half have responded with some level of commitment to Christ. Many have emigrated to Israel as zealous new believers. In Israel, they anticipate a major spiritual awakening as prophetic events unfold. In the meantime, they are quietly but faithfully proclaiming their Messiah to the Jewish nation. God is raising up a righteous remnant, a small but powerful contingent of Messianic believers in the Holy Land.

My husband, Scott, and I are in Odessa as short-term overseas workers on a gospel outreach to Jewish people like Leonid. It is our sixth such mission in two years. The outreach revolves around a city-wide festival of Hebraic style song and dance. Everyone in town has been invited to join us in worshipping the God of Israel.[1] The gospel is preached and opportunity is given to respond to the love of Jesus.

The Scriptures speak of such a time as this, when God will draw multitudes of Jews to their Messiah—and to their land:

> "'The days are coming,' declares the Lord, 'when men will no longer say, "As surely as the Lord lives, who brought the Israelites up out of Egypt," but they will say, "As surely as the Lord lives, who brought the Israelites up out of the *land of the north* and out of all the countries where He had banished them." For I will restore them to the land I gave their forefathers. But now I will send for many fishermen,' declares the Lord, 'and they will catch them. . .'"
>
> Jeremiah 16:14-15 (emphasis added)

According to the ancient text, the Jews' restoration from around the world begins in "the land of the north," a territory that biblical scholars generally agree refers to the geographic area north of Israel, i.e., the former Soviet Union, particularly Russia. This return will eclipse their exodus from Egypt. In fact, thus far, over 700,000 Jews from the former Soviet Union have emigrated to Israel since the collapse of the USSR.[2]

The Scriptures also speak of a "set time" for God to favor Zion—the Jewish people. That time is connected with nothing less than the glorious return of the Lord to the earth.[3] Jesus once told His disciples, "Behold the fig tree (symbolic of Israel) and all the trees. As soon as they put forth leaves, you see it and know for yourselves that summer is now near. Even so, you, too, when you see these things happening, recognize that the kingdom of God is near." (Luke 21:29-31 NAS; cf. Matthew 24:32-35, Mark 13:28-31.) Just what could this unprecedented outpouring of the Holy Spirit signal to the world, to the body of Christ and to Israel, whose acceptance of the Crucified One, according to Romans 11:15, means life from the dead? . . .

For the here and now, Leonid is proud of Odessa. Still called "Jewel of the Black Sea," this once ornate and cultured seaport city has shed much of its sparkle to poverty and disease. To Leonid, however, Odessa remains "beautiful" and "special." In typical Ukrainian manner, he has brought a gift for us this evening. Fingers fumbling with childlike excitement, he hands us an oversized bottle of Odessan chocolate liqueur. It is packaged in a box decorated on four sides with cityscape photos. No doubt it cost more than he could afford, but the Ukrainian people love to share or give away whatever little they have. It is definitely a distinctive gift for any missionary.

Leonid is glad we have come to Odessa. "Never has there been such a festival for Jewish people in this city," he tells us. "It is very, very good for the Jewish community. I hope it will come back every year." Hesitatingly, he adds, ". . . although I understand it is not so simple."

Our interpreter, a young Ukrainian believer with a passion for God and maturity well beyond her years, is the first to laugh at the suggestion. Leonid apparently has little understanding of the administrative hoopla involved, the seemingly endless stream of permits which had to be extracted from national, regional and local ex-Soviet bureaucrats. Perhaps he has also quickly forgotten about the opposition we faced from ultra-Orthodox Jewish sects. These so-called "anti-missionaries" caused such a stir with city officials and the local Jewish press that the festival was nearly canceled.

In any case, Leonid perceives that God has visited his city. "I do not consider myself to be a believer," he makes clear from the outset, "but I have deep respect for everyone who confesses religion of any form. I will explain why if you are interested."

A single light bulb dangling from the ceiling enables us to see how instantly solemn our guest has become. (Once more we are thankful for the electricity.) This is a man with a past that will not go away.

"Yes, of course, we are *very* interested," Scott and I reply in unison. How could we, two American Jews having no contact with this part of the world until just a couple of years ago, not be intensely interested? My own grandparents had come from Ukraine. Though they'd emigrated before the onslaught of the Soviet regime, I'd grown up on stories about "the old country." These stories were not filled with fond memories. They were tales of starvation, deprivation, fear and murderous anti-Semitism. Until recently, "the old country" had been shrouded in darkness and secrecy.

"Please tell us as much as you'd like," I add, straining to open an uncooperative window for fresh air so we can settle down comfortably for the evening. The window crank falls apart in my hands—screws, lever and all—yet another token of a world collapsing around us.

Leonid looks oddly surprised at our curiosity. It appears he is not used to an audience, and we can't help but wonder why. He takes a deep breath and begins haltingly, almost methodically, as if perusing well-maintained mental files.

"When I was eight years old, I was awakened once in the middle of the night by my father kissing me. The KGB (Soviet secret police) were in our house, taking my father away. We found out later they broke his back. My grandmother prayed to God that my father would not die. He lived and, when he came home, she believed more strongly in God. But I felt that if there was a God, why would He let these things happen to my father?

"The boys I knew said to me, 'Your parents are enemies of the state!' They beat me. This was in 1939, before the country was at war.

My father was a very honest man and a good man. I have still in my office one photo of my father and one of my mother. To me, they are like two icons.

"At first I judged Communism to be bad, an injustice. But then fascism came. We saw injustice there, too. We were all put in a ghetto camp, right here in Odessa. There were many terrible tortures and injustices. It was a long time ago, but still it is not easy for me to speak about.

"I did not understand about a normal childhood. I did not have it. I saw devout, elderly Jews who prayed all the time killed under terrible circumstances. Soldiers from Nazi armies came and took away pretty, young Jewish girls from their mothers.

"I hope to write a book about what happened in Odessa someday because I think most people do not know. Instead of taking us to concentration camps in Germany or Poland, the Nazis made a whole part of the city a ghetto camp for Jews. The same things that happened in the camps there happened here. I am getting old. It is a sad story but if I do not tell it, I do not think my children or grandchildren will tell it.

"I believe that if some Almighty Power exists, He cannot allow the things which I saw. I don't want to say this is 100 percent truth but, for me, it is my absolute conclusion. So now I cannot believe God created this world and would not put the right things in right places."

Leonid wipes his moistened brow and takes a moment to return to the present. His tone of voice, which reached peak crescendo prior to the pause, softens as he leans back on our steely sofa.

"I don't want you to think I came here tonight to antagonize you against God. I want to hear your opinions, too. Almost all believers are very kind, and I have a deep respect for all people who confess religion. I am like the bad product of atheism and socialism in this society. I have it through my parents and my grandparents, like a heritage. . ."

Heritage and tradition are important to the vast majority of Jews, even those in the former Soviet Union, where most religious activity was restricted for seventy years. The decades of atheism and suppression, combined with anti-Semitism, have had a predictable effect. Jewish identity is clouded and confused.

In the Western world, the Jewish psyche is largely shaped by what it is not—and it is decidedly not Christian.[4] Tragically, when Jews in the West look at the history of the church of Jesus Christ, what they see is mostly Jew hatred. Through that lens, they view a Jesus with a vendetta against them.[5]

Miraculously, most ex-Soviet Jews have been spared this view of Christianity. For others, like Leonid, sheer distance from the Father obscures sight of the Son. "It is like how I previously believed that all non-socialist countries and the people who lived there were bad," Leonid continues cautiously. "Not until the time of perestroika did people realize how much this was a lie. I didn't want to speak of politics, but it is very connected to our life here. I don't often speak of these things."

"May I respond?" Scott ventures.

"I will listen with great pleasure and then ask questions," Leonid replies, apparently relishing the freedom to openly exchange ideas, even disagreeable ones.

"You needn't worry about antagonizing us against God," Scott begins. "True faith in the true God is unshakable."

We talk of those tortured for their faith in Yeshua, such as Rev. Richard Wurmbrand, a Romanian Jew known around the world for his ministry to the persecuted underground church. Arrested in 1948 because of his commitment to Christ, Rev. Wurmbrand miraculously endured fourteen years in Communist jail cells. Somehow during those years, and while others in the same prison wondered where God was, Brother Wurmbrand experienced God's presence with him more than ever.

Together with Leonid, we ponder life's peculiar web of good and evil. It is a pattern, we tell him, formed from man's God-given ability to choose between the two. We speak of sin and its consequences, of suffering and how God can use even the most devilish for good. Our dialogue turns to heaven and hell, then to the Jewish people and their destiny.

"May I read you a short paragraph from the Jewish Scriptures?" I feel compelled to read a passage that has pressed on my spirit since we arrived in Odessa. It is one that seems to articulate the hushed heart cry of the Jews of that city.

Leonid nods approvingly. Despite all he has just said, he seems happy to have God's Word opened and explained to him. He strains to follow along in our translator's Russian Bible.

"Zion said, 'The Lord has forsaken me, and the Lord has forgotten me.' Can a mother forget her nursing child and have no compassion on the son of her womb? Even these may forget but I will not forget you. Behold, I have inscribed you on the palms of My hands; your walls are continually before Me." (Isaiah 49:15-16, NAS)

Leonid is visibly upset now. "I don't like this thing from the Bible. How can any mother forget about her own baby? It is another example of evil. If God exists, why would He let such a terrible thing happen?"

My thoughts instantly turn to the orphanages where Scott and I have been ministering in this city. Most of the children in these institutions are not there because their parents are dead. Most have simply been abandoned.

Four-year-old Liena captured our hearts the instant we met her. Her mother, like countless other citizens of the former Soviet Union, is an alcoholic with virtually no hope of recovery. Shortly after Liena was born, she handed her daughter over to an elderly woman to raise. The apparently kind but frail lady died only a couple of years later. A neighbor eventually saw to it that the girl got returned to her mother. Mom, however, lost no time in foisting her offspring upon yet another presumed caretaker. This individual apparently didn't want the waif either, however. She merely initiated legal proceedings so Liena could be officially declared abandoned and placed in an orphanage. All this time Liena's father managed to disclaim responsibility in the matter. Eventually he was arrested for an unrelated criminal offense and, by the time we met the child, he was serving time in jail.

Perhaps the greatest tragedy, as we saw it, was that Liena was an extraordinarily bright, sensitive and beautiful little girl. Her wide, crystal blue eyes hadn't yet lost their sparkle. When we handed her a new doll, it took her some minutes to realize it was hers to keep, then to recover from the giddy thrill of such a prize. Eventually, she found a secluded spot in the corner of a room and nestled down on the floor with her "baby," rocking it and softly singing an old Ukrainian lullaby, remembered from who-knows-where.

Given the grim realities of orphanage life, by the time Liena outgrows dolls, any God-given gifts will be hard to find. When she is a teenager, the system will turn her loose to fend for herself out on the streets. She will have no educational opportunities, no job, no family—just the bad product of a heritage, as Leonid would say. Another precious life crushed, unless the Master Himself intervenes.

Scott and I spent a long time with Liena. More than once we spoke to the authorities about adopting her. Ukrainian law, however, strictly prohibits foreign adoptions. The government says it is concerned that the children will be mistreated in other countries.

In a sense, Leonid is right: it is grotesquely unjust. A woman forgets her nursing child and has no compassion on the child of her womb. Indeed, the world without its Savior reeks of sin and evil.

God never told Job, the target of virtually every calamity imaginable, precisely why he suffered the way he did. Neither can we explain matters to Leonid. Ultimately and by divine intent, suffering defies rational explanation, beckoning in its stead sheer faith. It summons a faith which can flow only from a heart that bows to its Maker—a heart that, despite all else, knows and beats to His triumphant eternal love. In this kind of love, the Sovereign One designed even death and the devil and, in Christ Triumphant, Love Personified, He bids us to overcome, assured of an eternity thus ever more glorious.

It is getting late and Leonid must go home. Before he does, however, we extend hope to him one last time. Yet our friend's walls, built from atheism and cemented with sorrow, do not easily crumble. "We would like very much to pray for you before you leave and ask God to bless you. Would that be all right, Leonid?" I offer.

"Yes, of course!" he replies.

Paradoxically, Leonid seems just as eager for prayer as he was for Bible study. He says he felt as though God came close to him at the festival when there was prayer for salvation, and he wants to feel that again. "I want to pray right this time," he says, "so please tell me how."

The light bulb dangling from the ceiling is dimming and flickering, a sure sign the electricity will soon go out. We tell Leonid how: "Trust Him."

We ask the Spirit of God to bless Leonid with His promise from

Isaiah 49: "I will not forget you. Behold, I have inscribed you on the palms of My hands; your walls are ever before Me."

Leonid visibly tries not to cry. Holding back tears is no doubt a defense acquired decades ago, a once essential survival skill.

"Lord, would You show Leonid that his walls are always before You—but they have a built-in gate. Please give him the courage to unlock that gate for You someday."

Again and again, Leonid thanks us for the prayer. We escort him down to the hotel lobby, grateful that the elevators are still working. The evening, we all agree, has been much too short.

Scott and I watch our enigmatic guest step into the darkness outside, back into a no longer so God-forsaken life. Would Leonid ever believe the God of his fathers had visited him? We don't know. We only feel the Holy Spirit's bittersweet sign over his soul deposited on our hearts. We wonder if any of us will ever be the same. We hope not . . .

Time and again we'd seen the courage to believe dispensed to people like Leonid. There was Lida, for instance, whom I'd found a few months earlier sitting on a splintery bench in a scrubby park in Moscow. Under Stalin's brutal reign of terror, both she and her husband had been sentenced to the gulag (labor camp) for seventeen years. Her husband perished in prison. Lida was released, only to learn that her two children had been mysteriously murdered while she was away.[6] Somehow, Lida received the courage to open her heart wide to the love of Christ that day in the park.

Yakov, a Holocaust survivor living alone in a tiny flat in Minsk, Belarus, had escaped from Nazi hands by jumping off a train en route to one of Europe's notorious death camps, where the rest of his family lost their lives. Not until he met Yeshua, however, was Yakov able to escape the torment lingering in his soul since childhood. God used the tears of a Gentile member of our outreach team, shed literally at Yakov's feet in repentance for the sins committed against him, to crumble the walls about his heart.

We have been privileged to witness marvels in our day. We have seen multitudes, Jews and Gentiles together, come to faith rejoicing in the God of Israel. We've seen God begin to heal the effects of centuries of hatred and fear between them. As a result, governments initially set against the Lord have embraced a message of peace, comfort and hope.

We've seen Messianic Jewish congregations birthed throughout the former Soviet Union. Young leaders from these lands are being raised up to shepherd the flocks, then gather them back to Israel. It has been for us as in the days of the prophet Habakkuk, to whom God declared, "Look at the nations and watch—Be utterly astounded! For I will work a work in your days which you would not believe, though it were told you." (Habakkuk 1:5, NKJ)

Still, there are the Leonids and Lienas, and God will not forget them. Neither, therefore, can we. How long will these historically suppressed lands remain open to the gospel? No one knows for sure. As in the days of Isaiah, we only hear the Spirit say, "'Watchman, how far gone is the night?' The watchman says, 'Morning comes but also night. If you would inquire, inquire; come back again.'" (Isaiah 21:11-12, NAS)

That venerable inquiry and response frames the historical picture now unfolding halfway around the world. It is a picture of the Lord bringing treasures and riches out of the darkness, a darkness upon which a great light has shined.

A Harvest Field Found

"And this gospel of the kingdom will be preached in the whole world as a testimony to all nations, and then the end will come."

Matthew 24:14

WHEN GOD WANTS TO DO A NEW THING OF WIDESPREAD IMPACT, He often raises up a man and, through that man, begins the work. Respecting the sweep of Messianic Judaism among the one to five million Jews in the Commonwealth of Independent States,[7] that man is an affable and ardent Messianic Jewish pastor from Rochester, NY, named Jonathan Bernis.

Jonathan gave his life to Christ as a college student in upstate New York. Like many of his generation, in the late 1970s he was searching for truth in just about every place but the Bible. A friend who claimed Jesus had dramatically transformed her life persuaded him to visit a home Bible study in the spring of 1980.

Jonathan recalls that evening vividly. "I rode my motorcycle for miles in pouring rain to get to the Bible study. As soon as I arrived, I knew it wasn't for me. An older man greeted me by kissing me on the cheek and asking, 'Do you know Jesus?' With that, I tried to leave but the kind folks there insisted on running my soaking wet clothes through the dryer first. The Holy Spirit had me cornered. Somehow I ended up asking the Lord into my heart that night."

It took Jonathan some time to grasp the meaning of his salvation. "I'd come from a Jewish home and a synagogue background. I'd been taught the New Testament wasn't for me. I'd always thought Jesus was the son of Mr. and Mrs. Christ, and they'd lived in Rome. I never thought there was anything Jewish about it."

After receiving Messiah into his heart, however, Jonathan's theology changed rapidly and radically. He finished college with a degree in Judaic and Christian studies and, almost immediately, entered full-time ministry. Soon, he was respected throughout the Messianic Jewish movement as an impassioned visionary and incisive leader.

In the wake of glasnost, Jonathan grew increasingly burdened for the plight of the millions of Jews of the Soviet Union. For more than twenty centuries, their history had been fraught with tragedy. Disdained by the Orthodox Church fathers, then the czars and finally the Communists, Russian Jews had faced far more than the occasional, "polite" discrimination encountered in the West. Recurrently, whole Russian Jewish communities had been made to face, among other things, the choice of conversion to "Christianity" or death; slaughter from anti-Jewish, militia-led riots (called "pogroms") and extermination in labor camps. [8] It was in Russia that the so-called "Bible of Anti-Semitism," the infamous Protocols of the Elders of Zion, was concocted.[9] Alleging a secret international Jewish conspiracy to take over the planet, the Protocols, though found to be a forgery, have been cited by the Nazis, Arabs and other judeophobic hate groups around the world.

It has been remarked that anti-Semitism takes a predictable course. First a nation says, "You have no right to live among us as Jews." Next, it declares, "You have no right to live among us." Finally, that nation tells its Jews, "You have no right to live." Accordingly, death hangs over Jews in Soviet lands like a dragnet, periodically plunging for prey. At times hidden from view, its appetite is never appeased for long. Forever it wants more. . .of what it *doesn't* want at all!

Paradoxically, under Communism, countless numbers of Jews were denied the right to leave the USSR. Those daring enough merely to apply for emigration visas to Israel often endured cruel retaliation from the Communists.[10] They were not too unlike their ancestors of 3,400 years ago, subject to an Egyptian pharaoh who would not let them go.[11]

Jonathan wondered whether the situation might soon change. Recently he'd heard reports about spiritual hunger and openness to the gospel among the Soviet people. Behind the Iron Curtain lay fields ripe for harvest to a degree perhaps unparalleled in modern history. Was it possible the Spirit of God could be moving on the hearts of Soviet Jews as well?

It was 1989 when Jonathan first sensed the Lord 's stirring about a trip to the Soviet Union. He had always had a penchant for adventure; a personal fact-finding mission seemed the natural thing to do. In June 1990, the zealous young pastor landed himself, together with four daring American comrades, in the legendary city of Leningrad (now St. Petersburg).

In architectural design and layout, St. Petersburg is splendidly beautiful. To Jonathan and his scouting team, however, it was also dismal and dingy, its citizenry as depressed as most Western-drawn stereotypes. From all initial appearances, they couldn't help but agree with the Soviets' own assessment: "The great socialist experiment" had failed.

The morning after the group's arrival, Jonathan stared at the jet-lagged but trusting faces of his companions as they gathered in his hotel room. Just getting into the USSR had been such a challenge that he hadn't put together any specific plan for *after* they arrived. "God will lead," he kept telling himself and assuring the others.

Indeed, God had apparently led as they filed past airport officials and customs militia, their extra suitcases, stuffed with Bibles and gospel tracts, slipping by unnoticed. Collectively, however, the five Americans knew about fifteen words of Russian. Several phone calls earlier that morning had proved disappointingly fruitless. Jonathan had been able to reach none of the potential contacts he'd been given—except for two who spoke no English. The cumulative reality of no translator, no strategy and no personal acquaintances in this vast, far-flung *terra incognito* was hitting hard. There was nothing to do but pray.

"Help, Lord!" they cried. "We know You brought us here for a reason. Would You guide our steps? Please connect us to the Jewish people in this place and show us their hearts! We can do nothing without You."

Right after prayer, Jonathan tried again. This time, he happily reached Shalom, a Jewish architect-engineer who spoke English, more or less. Fortunately, he had a friend, Ana, a non-Jewish art professor who was fluent in the language.

Shalom and Ana would have been glad to spend time talking with any American, hearing their ideas and finding out about life in the United States. But conversing with American Jews who were also Christians—this, they agreed, was a most unusual and interesting opportunity, indeed! Shalom and Ana decided to take a few days off work to escort these folks around St. Petersburg, as well as translate, for the duration of their stay. God was faithful!

For the next three days, the team toured the city, distributing Bibles and literature wherever they went. No sooner would they give away a single Bible than a throng of spiritually starved Soviet citizens would surround them. With a desperation unknown in the West, old and young alike clamored for however many Bibles remained in the visitors' bags. The scene, repeated over and again, was dizzying. The Americans were puzzled. Where were all the atheists? Had seven decades of suppression backfired, resulting in a love for the Word of God beyond all imagination?

"Our people know they need God," said one pastor at a Baptist church Jonathan visited. "They now realize that a country without God will not have success."

Even as Jonathan and the pastor talked, a young man wandered in off the street, asking if anyone there could tell him about Jesus. To Jonathan's astonishment, the young man turned out to be Jewish. "He is not so unusual, brother," the pastor said. "Jews in Russia also want to know the truth about God. . ."

Jonathan spent most evenings that week having dinner with the families of contacts from abroad. As he quickly discovered, dinner in a Russian household is no simple affair. Most city dwellers live with extended family in small, three-room flats. One room is a tiny kitchen and another, a modest-sized bed chamber. The third, an inevitably cramped and cluttered space, serves as a dining/living area by day and sleeping quarters by night. On special occasions, the entire clan gathers around the dining table. Out of nowhere all kinds of prepared dishes appear: breads, borscht (a hearty beet or cabbage soup) potato and cabbage delicacies, meats, cheeses and fish. Butter and/or sour cream is a staple ingredient for most everything and helps one keep a healthy, rotund appearance. Sweet cakes and fancy cookies appear with tea for dessert. Despite widespread shortages of food and other supplies, (given way, in recent times, to lack of money instead) the people of the former Soviet Union will not skimp when it comes to hospitality. Like the widow in Jesus' day who could drop just two coins in the offering (Luke 21:1-4), they give sacrificially but all the more cheerfully, not from their abundance but from their lack. In God's eyes, theirs is the greater gift.

Jonathan exchanged stories with his hosts about American and Soviet Jewish life. In these tiny homes, he shared freely how he came to know the God of Israel through Jesus the Messiah. To his surprise, everyone seemed very interested. Many questions were asked. They wanted to know more . . . and more . . . and more! He couldn't help but think: "If only my congregation at home was so interested in my sermons . . ."

The second half of the week was spent in Moscow. Here the group had a more directed goal: to get Bibles and Messianic literature into the hands of those Jews seeking to emigrate to Israel, thus scattering spiritual seed into the Jewish State.

Following the Six Day War in 1967, the Soviet Union severed all formal diplomatic relations with Israel. As a result, exit visa applications to the Jewish State were processed as a courtesy through the Dutch Embassy in Moscow. The Dutch Embassy, Jonathan reasoned, would be as good a place as any to meet Jews moving to Israel, but neither he nor anyone else on the team knew where it was located. Again they prayed, hailed a taxi and trusted God for the rest.

For the next hour and a half, the team drove down nearly every major street in Moscow. Periodically, an animated exchange took place with the driver, relying heavily on exaggerated facial and upper body gestures. A sharp swerve in the opposite direction would inevitably follow. Eventually, the vehicle stopped, the driver proudly announcing the group's arrival at its destination. Hurriedly, he shuffled out his passengers, collecting and counting his rubles. Only after the car careened off to its next conquest did the group realize they were not at the Dutch Embassy.

Psalm 37:23 says the steps of a good man are ordered by the Lord. Thus Jonathan called it a "God-incidence" when a stranger overheard their dismayed conversation on the street and offered to escort them to the Dutch Embassy several miles away. The stranger, it turned out, not only worked at the Embassy; he was the dignitary directly responsible for processing emigration visas to Israel!

The Dutch consul personally ushered Jonathan's sleuths right into the Embassy compound, past a crowd of hundreds waiting outside locked gates. Once in his office, he explained in detail the situation of those Soviet Jews waiting to make *aliyah*. (To "make aliyah"—pronounced "ah-lee-yah" and meaning "ascent" in Hebrew— means to return to the biblical homeland.) The Dutch Embassy, the consul told them, was overwhelmed with Jews wanting to emigrate to Israel. The Soviet government had allowed only a few Israelis in to help process visas. The backlog, he sighed, was enormous. Over 49,000 applications had been filed since the beginning of that year. He pointed to a stack of papers a foot high. Of course, the Soviets would approve only a percentage of these for actual departure. He estimated an additional 15,000 visa applications would be submitted that month.

In recent weeks, nearly 2,000 Soviet Jews were emigrating each day, he said, in what was already being called "Operation Second Exodus." The numbers persisted despite the hurdles put up by the Soviets. The government required, for example, that an applicant depart within thirty days after a visa was issued. Since a visa may not be issued until months or years after it is applied for, this usually leaves only a couple of weeks for an entire family to prepare for the move. With them they may take a minimum amount of clothing, a wedding (but not an engagement) ring, and the equivalent of $50 in rubles. Often they lose their jobs and/or housing as soon as application papers are submitted. In addition, those emigrating to Israel immediately forfeit their citizenship and passports. Apparently, the Jews regard these obstacles as minor compared to the monumental lifting of the Iron Curtain itself. Jonathan's hunch was confirmed: the fulfillment of Jeremiah 16:14-15 had begun.

If God was the only One who could have arranged the chance meeting with the Dutch consul, only He could have known what awaited the group when they left his office. Walking out past the Embassy's gates, the five Americans began distributing Bibles and

Messianic literature to the 400 or so Jewish citizens lined up for aliyah applications. Within seconds, they were surrounded by a curious throng clamoring for more. Those fortunate enough to receive literature were soon swarming with questions, then kisses. Those who didn't get anything literally begged for a Bible or booklet. Others pleaded for a personal meeting at the hotel. Jonathan and his team had stepped into what was by far the ripest Jewish harvest field they'd ever seen! It was hard to tell who was the more delirious with delight: the Americans or the Soviets. For "when the Lord brought back the captives to Zion, we were like men who dreamed. Our mouths were filled with laughter, our tongues with songs of joy." (Psalms 126:1-2)

By now the KGB was tailing Jonathan by car. In the midst of the commotion, he hurried over to the parked automobile, motioned to the two men inside to roll down their window, and presented them with samples of smuggled gospel literature. Why should they be left out?

For the remainder of the day and into the night, the group excitedly shared about Yeshua, eventually giving away their own Bibles. The next morning they would fly back home, but Jonathan knew it was just the beginning . . .

Within several weeks of the group's return to the States, one of the many pamphlets distributed on the streets of St. Petersburg made its way several hundred miles southwest to Minsk, a medium sized city located in the Belarussian region of the USSR. There it fell into the hands of a Jewish believer named Volodya. Volodya promptly phoned the number printed on the back of the pamphlet, which connected him to a Messianic Jewish denominational organization in the US. "Would it be possible," he asked through an interpreter, "to send someone to Minsk to teach the people I pastor more about Messianic Judaism?"

In the fall of 1991, Jonathan was on his way once more to the Soviet Union to answer the pastor's plea. Accompanying him this time were two delegates from the denomination. To their surprise, the trio found a group of about seventy-five Jewish believers meeting every Sunday in a rented university lecture hall. They had a vision to form a congregation, focusing on outreach to the 75,000 or so Jews living in Minsk. Recently Volodya had placed an ad in a local paper inviting

Jewish people to a Bible study where they would receive a free copy of the Scriptures. Over 2,000 had come.

Jonathan had planned to spend much time sharing with Volodya and the group's elders about God's plan for Israel's restoration, both spiritually through salvation and physically through aliyah. To everyone's amazement, however, the Holy Spirit had already given the message. "We saw from chapters 9-11 in Romans," Volodya shared, "that it is God's will for Jewish people to be saved and this is possible only through Jesus Christ. Some people, Jews and non-Jews, think Jews can be saved another way, but this is not what the Bible says. There is only one way to our Father: through His Son. This is the New Covenant in Jeremiah 31, is it not?"

"We want to worship God as Jews," said the Belarussian worship leader. "In Romans 11, it says that all Israel will be saved. It also says that Gentiles who are saved are grafted into Israel, so we are one in the Lord, even though we are different nationalities. Yet when the New Covenant came, the Jews stayed zealous for the law, according to Acts 21:20."

"We also know," Volodya added, "that the Bible says a lot about the Jews in the Soviet Union because we are 'the land of the North.' We know God wants us to go to Israel as believers in Jesus. This is what He says in Jeremiah 16. We think if we do not go because we want to, He will send 'hunters.' Maybe this will mean terrible anti-Semitism and it will force us to go. But we would rather return freely, with joy. So, Brother Jonathan, can you help us? How is it we should live as Jews who love Jesus?"

Jonathan felt like a cork floating on an ocean. This move of the Spirit was more prodigious than he'd imagined. An isolated pocket cut off from the rest of the world, these leaders in Minsk had received the same revelation as had their Messianic brethren in America.

Over the next week, the delegation spent much time in Bible study, practical instruction, planning and prayer. The Belarussians learned Davidic-style worship and new songs in Hebrew. Clearly, however, a sovereign God had already imparted the same Messianic vision that had shaped the Jewish community of believers in the Western world for the past two decades.

God had also imparted to the Belarussian brothers the same heart. The Apostle Paul wrote, "I have great sorrow and unceasing grief in my heart. For I could wish that I myself were accursed, separated from Christ for the sake of my brethren, my kinsmen according to the flesh, who are Israelites, to whom belongs the adoption as sons and the glory and the covenants and the giving of the law and the temple service and the promises, whose are the fathers and from whom is the Christ according to the flesh . . ." The desire of Paul's heart and his unceasing prayer for them was that they might be saved. (Romans 9:2-5; 10:1, NAS)

With a passion not unlike Paul's, Volodya took Jonathan to visit the only remaining synagogue in Minsk. It was a small, wooden structure, seating perhaps fifty people, less than half of one percent of the city's Jewish population. But Volodya and Jonathan were not let in. Volodya was well known as a follower of Yeshua and, consequently, the religious leaders would have nothing to do with him.

Jonathan understood well the tears Volodya fought back at that moment. They came, first, from the synagogue's rejection of Messiah and, secondly, at the sting of being severed from his own people. This double "sorrow and unceasing grief" is shared by Jewish believers around the world. It is especially felt by those in the West where Jewish resistance to the gospel remains more the rule than the exception.

Many Gentile believers misunderstand this double burden, attributing it to misplaced sentimental or cultural ties. Such misunderstanding only compounds the Jewish believers' sense of alienation. As a result, they often feel cut off, not only from their "kinsmen according to the flesh," but from their spiritual brethren as well. So there was all the more reason to strengthen and encourage the fledgling flock in Minsk. Their challenge would be not to isolate and insulate themselves, but to bridge the local body of Christ with their own Jewish people . . .

The formal breakup of the USSR a few months later in December 1991 brought new opportunities for travel to some of its successor republics. Even former Soviet émigrés were now allowed back to visit. Such was the case with a friend of Jonathan's, a highly accomplished Messianic Jewish concert pianist, originally from Kiev. Together with another denominational delegate, the two plotted out an exploratory mission to Kiev, capital city of Ukraine, for the spring of 1992.

As usual the Lord opened doors to walk through, but just a step at a time. By a twist of circumstances, Jonathan's musician friend was able to hold an evangelistic mini-recital. Many Jewish people came and, at the end of the program, Jonathan shared the gospel. He then asked whether any would like to dedicate their lives to Christ. The response was so overwhelming and astonishing that the next step was clear. There would have to be a full-blown Messianic Jewish concert in Russia, festival-style, declaring Yeshua as the Savior of all!

On the return flight from Kiev, Jonathan knew God was speaking in a way that would alter the course of his life. While reading the Bible somewhere over Europe, he happened upon a familiar text, Jesus' teaching on the end of the age: "And this gospel of the kingdom will be preached in the whole world as a testimony to all nations, and then the end will come." (Matthew 24:14).

Jonathan jumped in his seat. The passage stood out to him in a way that he had never seen before. The Greek word translated as "nations" in that passage, he remembered, was "ethnos," meaning ethnic or people groups. The biblical reference here, he realized in a flash, was not to geo-political boundaries but to *people!* "I am not so concerned," the Lord impressed on him, "with land masses as I am with the souls of men." Biblically, the Jewish people form a distinct "ethnos," regardless of where they live. It struck him that, while many missionaries had been sent out to the ripe harvest fields of the former Soviet Union, few, if any, were laboring specifically with the Jewish people. He knew that, to reach the Jews as a group anywhere, the gospel must be presented in a Jewish context. Thus, the Jews behind the shattered Iron Curtain were a whole mission field within a mission field!

He hurriedly flipped back in his Bible a few hundred pages. "But now I will send for many fishermen. . .and they will catch them." Jonathan had read this verse from Jeremiah 16 countless times in the past two years. There was something, however, he had never realized before: Jesus referred to evangelists as fishermen![12] "And they will catch them," the Scriptures said. During these three trips to the CIS, he had shared the gospel and prayed with more Jewish people than in ten full years of Jewish ministry in the United States. The fishermen of Jeremiah 16 are evangelists *guaranteed* a catch!

In October 1992, the now itinerant Messianic pastor again flew to St. Petersburg. There he found a hotel room and began praying. Over the next few days, the Holy Spirit revealed a specific strategy for a musical outreach festival in that city to proclaim salvation in the name of Yeshua. The steps, still coming just one at a time, were getting bigger and riskier. Jonathan had barely an inkling of where or how it would end. But he would obey.

The basic battle plan was to "let Judah go up first," breaking spiritual ground through celebrative praise and Davidic-style worship. Jonathan spent the better part of the next year coordinating a city-wide festival, featuring Messianic musicians from the United States and Europe. After the concert, he would share from his personal testimony, present the gospel and see what happened.

The Messianic Jewish Festival of St. Petersburg in May 1993 was no small undertaking. The organizational details seemed endless. Russian red tape was like nothing Jonathan had ever encountered before. (What can be accomplished in an hour in America generally takes a full day in Russia—if it can be done at all.) Adding to the administrative and bureaucratic gymnastics was the recruitment and coordination of nearly 100 volunteer team members from Europe and the US.

None of those who invested time and money to participate in that first festival really knew what to expect. They had all come in faith, serving either on street outreach, round-the-clock intercessory prayer, administrative, or technical/performance teams. The street outreach teams were quick to report great openness among the people and many instances of divine physical healings. Intercessory prayer had gone well. Nonetheless, the night before the first concert, Jonathan lay wide awake, unable to sleep. A nagging scene played over and again in his mind: himself, standing center stage, outfitted in his new suit, preaching his heart out to a huge hall—with two full rows of seated onlookers, every one of them the politely smiling members of his team. The whole while he preached, he worried how he would ever find the words to apologize to the musicians who'd rearranged their busy schedules to accommodate his latest spiritual whims.

As it turned out, approximately 12,000 Russians attended the festival over a three-night period. Many more who came were unable to squeeze into the concert hall, which seated only 4,000. Each night, after the worship, Jonathan shared about his own spiritual pilgrimage. Then he told the people about Jesus:

"The reason all of us came here and put on this performance for the city free of charge is that we believe it tells the most important message anyone can hear. It is the message that God sent His Messiah to the Jewish people, and to the rest of the world, and His name is Yeshua, or Jesus.

"The Bible has many prophecies that predict things that would happen long before they actually came to pass. This is one reason we know the Bible is from God and that it is true. One of the Jewish prophets, Jeremiah, said that, as long as there was a sun to shine by day and a moon to shine by night, and as long as there were stars shining in the sky, God would preserve the Jewish people as a nation. It's no coincidence that, even with Communism trying to stomp out religious identity, God preserved you as a Jew. His Word promised it.

"You have the freedom now to choose for yourself whether to believe the Bible or not. You've served others long enough. You've served the system long enough and it failed you. Now God says, 'Serve Me. I will never fail you.' "

Jonathan watched people lean forward in their seats and listened to the hush that descended on the crowd.

"If you want to serve God, you must give Him your life. The Bible says that God created us to have a relationship with Him, to live in His love, peace and joy. But we have all broken His laws and that's called sin. Once we sin, we can no longer be in relationship with Him. Instead, we are separated from Him in this life and in eternity. But because God loves us so much, He sent His Son, Jesus, to take to the cross in His own body the penalty for all our sins. You can be forgiven for all your sins, now, by believing in Yeshua.

"God offers you this free gift, the gift of His forgiveness, love and eternal life. Your life on earth is very short and often filled with suffering. But this is nothing compared to the endless suffering for those who die without their sins being forgiven. If you want this free gift, if you are willing to commit your life to Yeshua as the One you serve and want to ask Him into your heart, please come down to the front of the auditorium. It doesn't matter if you are Jewish or not. God loves you and wants to give you this free gift."

Each time Jonathan gave an altar call, hundreds ran down to the platform to pray with him and ask Jesus into their hearts. Of that number, well over half were Jewish. The place was electrified. Nobody there had ever before seen anything like it. God did abundantly beyond what they had hoped! Jonathan and his workers were jubilant!

"'He who scattered Israel will gather them and will watch over His flock like a shepherd.' For the Lord will ransom Jacob and redeem them from the hand of those stronger than they. They will come and shout for joy on the heights of Zion; they will rejoice in the bounty of the Lord . . ." (Jeremiah 31:10-12)

A Messianic Jewish congregation was immediately launched to disciple the new believers. Once each month, Jonathan flew from Rochester, NY, to St. Petersburg, Russia, to conduct *Shabbat* (Hebrew for "Saturday Sabbath") services. Hundreds came to each meeting and many others made first-time professions of faith.

Jonathan agonized in prayer for the Lord of the harvest to find and send mature leadership to the nascent congregation. It wasn't long before he heard the inevitable: "Why don't you go? Why don't *you* move to St. Petersburg and pastor them?" The Holy Spirit spoke gently but plainly to his heart.

In September 1993, Jonathan resigned from his pastorate in Rochester, sold his house and moved to Russia. By then, the largest Messianic Jewish congregation in the non-Western world was flourishing. One year later, the first Messianic Jewish Bible school in the former Soviet Union opened its doors in St. Petersburg to 120 students. Jonathan's vision, by the Spirit of God, was two-fold: to raise up mature leadership for Messianic congregations throughout the former Soviet Union, and to commission young Russian Jews who were on fire for Yeshua to make aliyah and impact the nation of Israel.

In the meantime, something had to be done while the doors were open to reach the many thousands of Jews in other cities in the former Soviet bloc. There would have to be more grace, more prayer, more resources, more workers and more festivals.

Moscow: Blessing a Desolate House

"Oh Jerusalem, Jerusalem, you who kill the prophets and stone those sent to you, how often I have longed to gather your children together as a hen gathers her chicks under her wings but you were not willing. Look, your house is left to you desolate. For I tell you, you will not see me again until you say, 'Blessed is he who comes in the name of the Lord.'"   Matthew 23:37-39

THE FIRST TIME I FLEW TO THE FORMER SOVIET UNION, I did not have to be told when our jetliner crossed into Russian airspace. I could feel it. Something like an ethereal soul cry hangs over the vast bleak stretches of dreary brown soil below. It issues up to the heavens like collective lament that has loudened over the centuries. It is a spiritually palpable plea for help, one which God certainly hears: "'Because of the oppression of the weak and the groaning of the needy, I will now arise,' says the Lord. 'I will protect them from those who malign them.'" (Psalms 12:5)

It was the spring of 1994. Scott and I were going to Moscow as part of the ministry team for the second International Messianic Jewish Festival. We were excited, of course, and maybe even a bit nervous. I recalled the legends my bubby ("grandmother" in Yiddish) used to recount about "the old country." My favorite was the one about how she slipped out of Russia at age 16 by hiding in a hay wagon. Once across the border, she boarded a ship and sailed, most courageously I thought, to an unknown world offering such strange things as freedom and hope. I always wanted more details but she never supplied them. "Better you should never have to know," she would sigh.

But her clandestine accounts only served to pique my curiosity. I had inherited something from that obscure past, whether or not I could ever comprehend it. So how mind-boggling it was to at last visit this far-flung and oddly alluring place—commissioned with a message of the freedom and hope to be found, not in a country new or old, but in Messiah Jesus!

Once on the ground and en route to the city, our team gleaned its first impressions of Russia. Shock quickly rippled through our ranks. Is this the country America was so afraid of for so long? Granted, nuclear arms were supposedly stockpiled all over the former Soviet empire. But from the vantage point of our bus window, we were appalled at the evidence of widespread poverty: decrepit buildings, broken-down vehicles and roadside machinery, unbridled pollution and dirt, and people clothed in rags.

Even worse than its structural dilapidation, the former Communist capital appeared caught in a tailspin of disorder. Angry confusion marked virtually every human interaction, from traffic on the highways to personal encounters on street corners, to our hotel check-in (which took approximately three hours). How much of the disarray was the result of recent political and socio-economic upheaval and how much had, in fact, made perestroika inevitable? Job 12:23 says, "He makes nations great and destroys them; He enlarges nations and disperses them." The life and death of the Soviet empire was ultimately God's doing.

It was during the country's famed "white nights" that our mission would take place. Since it is so far north, Russia experiences sunset very late during the summer—near midnight in Moscow, followed by an early morning sunrise. Further north, in St. Petersburg, the sun does not completely set for weeks at a time. Tourists find this aberration of nature exhilarating. The opposite, of course, happens in winter. Then the days are very short and the nights long and dark. The phenomenon of nature reflects well the region's spiritual climate.

Like a celestial white night, the spiritual awakening in the former Soviet Union has been unlike anything the modern world has known. Few places have been so historically replete with darkness and death. Nowhere has a political system so grounded on the non-existence of

God and so dedicated to the suppression of truth remained in power over so broad a geographic territory. As certainly as night follows day, however, the Russian peoples are not free from darkness' supernormal return. All the more reason to labor, as Jesus said, while the light of day remains.

At our first team meeting in Moscow, we met some of those willing laborers. From all over North America, Europe, Israel and Russia, 275 Gentile and Jewish believers from various church streams convened, ready for battle. Each had volunteered to work in one of five areas: administration, intercession, outreach, technical/performance or translation. They represented a veritable cross-section of the body of Christ.

Huddled together in a poorly lit, poorly heated and barely ventilated hotel meeting hall, this unique work force consisted mostly of lay people gladly sacrificing their personal savings and vacation time to be there. They had come together for one overriding purpose: to serve Jesus together and, over the next week, make known His salvation. It was an army!

That war had been declared long ago was already apparent to us. In the past twenty-four hours we'd seen the beautiful but beaten-down faces of the Russian people. Sullen eyes and drooping heads reflected the vicissitude of victimized lives. It was as if an entire population had been so whipped, it had forgotten how to smile. Huge crowds hurried along robotically in the damp, gray chill. (Never mind that it was late spring; the temperature registered all of 35 degrees Fahrenheit.) Seventy years of Communism had apparently left as its legacy a people in search of a soul. Life was reduced to a daily struggle to survive, out of which a veneer was drawn that scarcely covered a percolating national rage.

This struggle to survive could be observed outside most any of the city's busy subway stations. Moscow's Metro in and of itself is legendary. Aptly described as an underground museum, this elaborate train system was obviously built in a bygone era of relative prosperity. Walnut and marble walls and pillars, majestically engraved, line its corridors. Crystal chandeliers hang every hundred feet or so from high, carved ceilings, making the subway the most brightly lit place in the city. Socialist insignia and murals decorate the tunnels to inspire the working masses. Revolutionary soldiers, cast in marble and bronze, stand sentinel throughout the palatial labyrinth.

The Muscovites were understandably proud of their subterranean showcase. To their credit, they managed to keep the whole subway system immaculately litter-free and polished. Graffiti was entirely non-existent. (This later became a problem for us when those opposed to our message threw their festival tracts down on the floor. They knew the police would soon evict us and arrest the team leaders for littering in the Metro.)

The scene outside many of the Metro stations contrasted sharply with the splendor downstairs. A dozen or more peddlers, mostly middle aged and elderly women, stood all day long, displaying their wares. Staring blankly at the endless throngs of passers-by, they held in their hands a single item or two for sale, such as a clock, a cooking utensil, a couple of plastic flowers, a pair of sneakers, a puppy or kitten—the animal inevitably presenting the same impassive stare. On a good day, one of their pathetic items might get sold for a dollar (except for the purebred pets, which brought in a lot more). These were not street people but rather, for the most part, retired pensioners. Once respected Soviet workers, they now fell haplessly through the cracks of economic restructuring. Hawking their personal possessions was the only way they knew to supplement a pitifully low fixed income, and eke out some form of existence.

Located in the same flea market-like arena as the peddlers was an amorphous array of brightly pained kiosks. Most of them, new since capitalism, were well stocked with American-brand candy bars and soft drinks, as well as gum and cigarettes. Most also boasted one or two boxes of facial tissue, a few fancy pencils, a dozen heavy metal music tapes and random items like one flashlight, one transistor radio or one battery—that would not be the right type for either the flashlight or the radio. It was a puzzling display.

These were the highways and byways in which we would issue half a million invitations to the Master's banquet: "Come all you who are thirsty. . . and you who have no money, come, buy and eat!" We prayed especially hard that the city's 250,000-plus Jews might be, in Jesus' words, compelled to come.

We'd heard all the exciting reports from last year about St. Petersburg. But we didn't know quite what to expect in Moscow, a different place with different people. We were cautioned that many Muscovites, overwhelmed with an influx of spiritual and cultic information, were not so open any more, either to the Lord or to foreigners. So it was with both exhilaration and anticipation at the immensity of the task that we submerged ourselves in the masses of the marketplace.

The crowds on the streets of Moscow were enormous. Predictably, we were not met with the desperate curiosity of one or two years ago. Nevertheless, waves of willing recipients vacuumed our tract bags clean. Keeping our supply of invitations in tow with demand proved the challenge of the day. In the cold weather, our hands and fingers soon ached from the constant exertion — and we celebrated! Almost everyone to whom it was offered took a festival invitation, which contained a gospel message on its reverse side. Many stopped in their tracks to read it and many more were eager to talk. Some put their faith in Jesus right then and there. It was thrilling and bewildering at the same time!

Our last day out before the festival, we decided to put on a mini-gospel concert in one of Moscow's busier shopping districts. All week long, we'd delayed the event, hoping the weather would warm up. Finally we concluded we would just have to tough it out in the cold.

The ministry began with two Jewish pastor-evangelists, one from Israel and one from Maryland, proclaiming boldly that the Bible, God's book of truth, teaches salvation in Christ alone. To my relief, nobody tried to arrest us; rather, they flocked politely and expectantly around to listen. People were genuinely interested!

Just when I wondered if the USSR had somehow become the "land of the free," a lottery ticket salesman with megaphone in hand spotted the crowd. Because of the preaching, dozens of potential customers had converged on his street corner. The enterprising young man seemed determined to break the sound barrier, if need be, to get the crowd's attention and hawk his goods.

"Not to worry," the unfazed American evangelist assured everyone. In typical Russian free-market style, he simply "purchased" the megaphone—$10 for an hour's use—a windfall for the lottery dealer. After that, our friend was content to sit quietly for the next hour and let some of his countrymen get saved.

We had another problem, however, when it became apparent the musicians were not going to join us on the streets as had been planned. (They were concerned that the freezing weather would wreak havoc with their vocal cords.) Rather than cancel the show, the resourceful Israeli brother promptly deputized the rest of us "the choir." Our rag-tag band sang its heart and soul out, sometimes on key. To make up for the music, the two evangelists resumed preaching until they both lost their voices, megaphone notwithstanding.

At that point and for the rest of the afternoon, the street ministry was turned over to the translator, a young Muscovite who could better withstand the effects of the cold on her respiratory tract. In addition, impassioned little Sasha had no use for voice amplification. "Today is the day for salvation!" she bellowed out unabashedly. "Old ideology is gone. It is an idol that has toppled. Only Jesus lives forever!" Within minutes, another plentiful harvest was gathered in. Our heads were spinning, our hearts leaping.

Compared to evangelism in the West, ministry in Moscow was like walking in zero gravity—no resistance—until the unexpected happened.

While the Russian people expressed no hostility at the proclamation of the gospel of Jesus Christ, many folks were thoroughly enraged at our publicly representing and, worse yet, doing, something Jewish. Oddly, the hunched-over, gray-haired *babushkee* (Russian for "grandmothers") were the most infuriated.

At first I was eager to hand these little old ladies my tracts, expecting to find them the kindly old matrons they looked to be.

"Jew, go home!" shrieked one. The mere sight of the word, "Jewish," on the invitation had horrified her. She tore it up into little pieces in front of me, hurled it to the ground, then spit all over the shredded document and left muttering in great distress.

"Jewish? I hate Jews! They should all burn in hell for what they have done!" another old woman shouted, her fists shaking wildly in the air. Then she launched into a polemic on how the Jews were to blame for all the ills of her beloved country.

The useful phrase, *"Ya nye goveroo Parooski"* ("I don't speak Russian") eventually put an end to her fit. In the meantime, I took advantage of the curiosity of passers-by to distribute more invitations. But it wasn't long before I managed to arouse the wrath of another wrinkled little babushka.

"Festival for Jews? *You Jews are pigs*! You are devils!" she cried.

I finally stopped asking for translations, while my Russian co-laborer seized the opportunity to preach about the love of Jesus, a Jew, for all peoples. I, however, was dumbfounded. The babushkee, everyone said, were among the most devout attendees of the Russian Orthodox Church, that singular institution that has managed to outlive every political regime—the early monarchs, the czars and even the Communists. So shouldn't they be pro-evangelistic and reflect Christian love?

Some of my co-workers were not as fortunate as I. For whatever reasons, those targeted for bodily assault were the Gentile team members. (Of course the enemy usually attacks those who dare to ally with the Jews.[13]) One angry man grabbed a friend of mine, a petite, attractive woman from Maryland. With a venomous hatred she'd never experienced before, he punched her in the jaw, pushed her against a brick wall and spat on her. Yet another pint-sized but gutsy sister from West Virginia felt certain she was about to be smacked in the head when a young man threw his invitation to the ground, hollering "Heil Hitler" in her face. Not knowing whether he spoke any English, she locked eyes with him and calmly replied, "God bless you." He walked away. One good brother from Indiana was assaulted by a gang of seven neo-Nazis. We praised God nobody was seriously hurt but, on account of such incidents, security guards were hired for all festival-related activities.

To what extent could Russia in the mid-nineties be compared to pre-World War II Germany? In these years of economic hardship, political instability and moral uncertainty, unhealed wounds and old hatreds have risen to the fore in search of a scapegoat. Hitler offered the beleaguered Germans a package of moral improvement and ethnic cleansing, wrapped in the platitudes of economic reform.[14] Fanatical and increasingly popular Russian ultra-nationalists, such as Vladimir

Zhirinovsky, now promise much the same. As far as these pundits are concerned, the Jews are again to blame.[15]

The Orthodox Church has, in its official capacity, done little if anything to counter Jew hatred in Russia. To the contrary, the institutional church has only helped solidify anti-Jewish sentiment.

In the tenth century, Prince Vladimir of Kiev Rus, the territory from which Russia and other Slavic nations sprang, embraced Orthodox Christianity and made it the religion of the state.[16] At the same time, he decried any and all remaining vestiges of Judaism.[17] Under his influence, the patriarchs of Russian Orthodoxy soon became known for their explicitly anti-Jewish writings.[18]

Founding fathers St. Cyril of Turov and Hilarion of Kiev, for instance, renounced the Jews as a divinely repudiated race, superseded in the plan of God by believing Gentiles and, in particular, Russians.[19] The notion evolved that Jews would inevitably corrupt Russian Christians if allowed to live in proximity to them.[20] This presented a problem, never fully solved, since so many Jews lived within the Russian empire. For a time, all Jews were confined to certain delineated areas of the former Soviet lands, called the Pale of Jewish Settlement.[21]

As a byproduct of this ideology-theology, Jews living in Russia are not, even to this day, considered to be Russians.[22] If a Jew wishes to be regarded and treated as a Russian, which is rarely an option, he must totally renounce his Jewish heritage. In any event, the tenets of church fathers like Hilarion and Cyril remain foundational to the faith and continue to influence Russian thought and culture.[23] Twentieth century church writings still blame Russia's problems on the Jews.[24]

At its inception, the Russian Orthodox Church learned it would not survive without special favor from the government. Since the early monarchs, down through the centuries of czardom and up through the catechism of Communism, Russian Orthodoxy has maintained a formal alliance with the political powers that be.[25] Inevitably, Russian nationalism came to be ingrained in the very woof and warp of the church. For centuries, church and state dogma held to Moscow as the Third Rome or New Israel.[26]

Even the Communists realized early on that it would be better to keep some semblance of the church around, serving Party purposes, than to obliterate it altogether. For seventy years, the KGB made sure only those churches cooperating fully with the state retained the right to exist. Full cooperation meant staying out of politics or any issues of social concern. In effect, it meant intimidating parishioners into tacit submission to authority.[27]

Orthodox doctrine and practice, however, lent itself comparatively well to such a task. For example, according to the church, spiritual authority is vested exclusively in the ordained clergy, not the ordinary believer. Salvation is based on baptism in the church and obedience to the priest. Church icons and paintings are not merely sacred art; they are as revered as the Scriptures. Parishioners may observe but not participate in the highly liturgical services which last several hours at a time and are usually conducted in an old Slavonic language incomprehensible to most Russians.[28]

In this religious context, latent elements survived that would fuel the ultra-nationalists' ideology as soon as the Soviet regime collapsed. The communists, after all, were in power for only seventy years, whereas the nationalists trace their roots back over a millennium. A sympathetic audience would be at hand; in 1996, seventy percent of Russians identified themselves as affiliated with the Russian Orthodox Church.[29]

The above discussion is not intended as a polemic against Russian Orthodoxy. In spite of seemingly insurmountable opposition, that church is to be credited for keeping some modicum of Christianity alive in the former Soviet Union. Within its ranks there has always been a remnant faithful to God. Many of these saints suffered tremendously for their faith. The body of Christ in the Western world can hardly fathom the price paid by some of these martyrs.[30] They and the Communist-era underground body of believers[31] are to be highly esteemed. Nonetheless, the Russian Orthodox Church as a whole has failed to demonstrate God's love toward the Jewish people.

The fruit of this failure is evidenced in splinter groups such as *Pamyat*. Pamyat means "memory." Pamyat remembers, and is dedicated to the restoration of, the czarist monarchy. It is watched by Jewish organizations around the world because of its anti-Semitic agenda and recent acts of violence.[32] It has claimed responsibility for, among other things, the burning of synagogues and desecration of Jewish cemeteries throughout Russia. Heretofore, Pamyat had not been willing to talk with leaders of the Jewish community.

When the Messianic Jewish Festival came to town, the organization was quick to issue threats of violence against it. We were publicly promoting something Jewish, i.e., not Russian. We were promoting a Jewish Jesus. We were a direct challenge to "Memory!"

As the week went on, however, Pamyat's leader, Dmitri Vasilyev, expressed an interest in meeting with Jonathan. The idea of a face-to-face exchange had been proposed by a Moscow journalist looking for a story. Initially, Jonathan was reluctant to take time out of his busy schedule. He had little desire to engage in discourse with the known authors of hate and brutishness. He was willing, however, to pray about it.

"This is good and pleases God our Savior, who wants all men to be saved and to come to a knowledge of the truth." First Timothy 2:4 kept turning over in Jonathan's mind. He knew the Lord wanted even Vasilyev and his men to be saved and come to a knowledge of the truth. He conceded to talk to them, purposing not to debate the merits of anti-Semitism, but to preach the gospel and give them an opportunity to repent.

Pamyat's offices were housed in an ordinary apartment building distinguishable only by its iron gates and black-uniformed, armed guards. On the afternoon of their arrival, Jonathan and the two Messianic pastors accompanying him were taken upstairs—to a throne room. Together with the journalist who'd arranged the meeting, all were seated at a long, wooden table. On an elevated platform at the head of the table stood an ornately carved mahogany throne. Portraits of the czars, including Nicholas, Peter the Great, Nicholas II—and Vasilyev—hung above the royal seat. Icons and other czarist memorabilia filled the dimly lit chamber. After several minutes, in came Vasilyev's forerunners: his personal Russian Orthodox priest, decked in flowing robes and jewels, and an armed bodyguard. Next, Vasilyev made his entrance. Outfitted in blouson trousers and shirt, wide belt and boots, he indeed looked the part of a peasant populist general-who-would-be king. Vasilyev ascended his throne.

Jonathan would not be intimidated. "We are here to talk about the gospel of King Jesus, our Messiah," he said.

A long talk followed. Vasilyev and his priest insisted God no longer had a plan of blessing for the Jewish people. "We are not anti-Semitic," they offered in defense. "It is simply that Jews have destroyed this country. They will destroy any country. But not you. You are good Jews. Our Bible says that, before Christ returns, some good Jews will believe in Him. Because of this, we thought you would understand our position."

Did these Pamyat pretenders really expect Messianic Jews to sympathize with their cause? Had they seriously entertained the notion of some unholy alliance with them? Stripped of its surrealistic pageantry, the scene playing itself out was an all too familiar one.

The Pamyat priest was not the first to interpret the Scriptures so as to replace Israel as the people of God with the church. Under "replacement" or "transfer" theology, all the covenantal and prophetic blessings of God have been transferred from Israel to the church. Any present or future application of blessing to Israel is replaced by, and fulfilled in, the church. The Jewish people do retain something of a biblical inheritance, replacement pundits say, namely, all the curses.[33] Having rejected their Messiah, the Jews are forever destined to doom themselves and all those around them. Threads of replacement doctrine run throughout the root system of Russian Orthodoxy and its offshoots.

It is important to understand replacement doctrine because it has so significantly shaped the religious context in which God's Spirit is moving on the Jews of the former Soviet Union. Just as important, replacement doctrine has over the centuries influenced much of the church worldwide to varying degrees. Where it has gained a toehold, it has resulted in little or no value being placed on Jewish evangelism. Where it has gained a foothold, it has led to the church's expelling from its ranks born-again Jews who refuse to renounce their ethnic heritage. Where it has gained a stronghold, replacement doctrine has fueled the attempted annihilation of the Jewish race. Genocide is the "logical" final outcome for those cursed ones opposing Christ and the extension of His kingdom.

Different forms of replacement doctrine can be found in many churches around the world, including America.[34] These churches fail to understand that those who bless Israel will be blessed, but those who curse her will be cursed. In addition, Christians who believe God would renege on His promises to Israel must be left in perpetual doubt as to the security of their own relationship with the Father. If the Jews could fall irreparably from grace, could not also the church?

Those who would replace ethnic Israel with the church do not understand the biblical basis for God's continued covenant relationship with the Jewish people. Certainly the Bible teaches that everything it says concerning Israel has applicability to the body of Christ. "All Scripture is God-breathed and is useful for teaching, rebuking, correcting and training in righteousness, so that the man of God may be thoroughly equipped for every good work." (II Timothy 3:16) Accordingly, believing Gentiles participate in and fully enjoy all the blessings of salvation given to Israel. (Ephesians 3:6; Romans 11:17)

At the same time, the Father has destined a specific course for Abraham's physical seed which He has yet to fulfill and which cannot be usurped. From the outset, God's covenant to Abraham and his lineal descendants, first stated in Genesis 12:1-3, 7, is *unconditional*:

> "The Lord had said to Abram, 'Leave your country, your people and your father's household and go to the land I will show you. I will make you into a great nation and I will bless you; I will make your name great, and you will be a blessing. I will bless those who bless you, and whoever curses you, I will curse; and all peoples on earth will be blessed through you....to your offspring I will give this land."

The fulfillment of this promise is dependent on nothing other than God's own Word. It cannot be nullified. In Genesis 15, God unilaterally seals His promise to Abraham in the covenant-solemnizing ceremony then typical of the ancient Middle East. As a result, Israel's obedience to the Lord, or lack thereof, is, in this instance, irrelevant to the fulfillment of His covenant with them. In fact, it is precisely because of Israel's unfaithfulness that God says He will make a New Covenant with them (Jeremiah 31:31-33). Even so, the Abrahamic Covenant and its continued applicability to Israel is reaffirmed throughout the Old and New Testaments.[35]

The Bible makes clear that salvation is possible only through personal faith in Jesus Christ. Jews who do not believe in and personally embrace Yeshua as Messiah enjoy no special privileges. They do not partake of the blessings of salvation. Nonetheless, God has a distinct plan for Israel's restoration as a whole. That restoration, which has already begun in part, is both physical—returning to the land of Israel—and spiritual— turning in repentance to Messiah.

To disclaim God's Word or heart of love and grace toward Israel is to "boast against the branches," about which the Apostle Paul warns:

> "And if some of the branches were broken off and you, being a wild olive tree, were grafted in among them, and with them became a partaker of the root and fatness of the olive tree, do not boast against the branches. But if you boast, remember that you do not support the root but the root supports you. You will say then, 'Branches were broken off that I might be grafted in.' Well said. Because of unbelief, they were broken off and you stand by faith. Do not be haughty but fear. For if God did not spare the natural branches, He may not spare you either….And they also, if they do not continue in unbelief, will be grafted in, for God is able to graft them in again." (Romans 11:17-23, NKJ)

Replacement doctrine can find fertile ground in a heart of pride or, conversely, insecurity of the order described by Paul. It is usually defended theologically by a method of Bible interpretation that is allegorical or non-literal, and presumes the Scriptures mean something other than what they plainly state. This allegorical school of thought was developed in the third century in Alexandria, Egypt, a city then regarded as a world center for anti-Semitism.[36] The new approach was specifically intended to reconcile the New Testament with Greek philosophy and remove its Jewish essence. It sought also to rationalize away the supernatural elements of difficult biblical passages.[37]

An allegorical approach to interpreting the Bible relies heavily on symbolism. Certainly the Scriptures do make use of symbols but, unlike the methods of Bible interpretation commonly accepted in the evangelical church since the Protestant Reformation,[38] strict allegorists do not aim to attribute to the words of Scripture their plain and ordinary, literal meaning. Neither the ordinary rules of grammar, nor the historical-cultural environment in which a biblical text was written, is necessarily considered.

Allegorically interpreting the Bible, St. Augustine, a leading church father of the fifth century,[39] wrote his famed treatise, "The City of God." In it, he concluded God was finished with the Jews. The church was not only Israel's replacement; the body of Christ was called, he believed, to ensure her humiliation and revocation of grace.[40] Augustine's teaching became a central tenet of the church. After all, Israel had been dispersed as a nation for centuries. Gentile believers could see no tangible evidence of blessing on the physical sons and daughters of Jacob. Unresolved prophecies about the Jews must pertain now to them instead.

One of the deficiencies, however, of an allegorical interpretation of Scripture is that difficult passages are not considered within the context of the Bible as a whole.[41] Accordingly, replacement doctrine hones in on certain verses viewed in isolation and out of context. In effect, it then reinterprets the Bible as a whole, based on those select passages.

One such passage is Romans 2:28-29:

> "A man is not a Jew if he is only one outwardly, nor is circumcision merely outward and physical. No, a man is a Jew if he is one inwardly; and circumcision is circumcision of the heart, by the Spirit, not by the written code. Such a man's praise is not from men but from God."

From this verse, replacement adherents draw the conclusion that believing Gentiles are now the true Jews. What Paul in this context is saying, however, is that among ethnic Jews, those not inwardly circumcised are not spiritual Jews, i.e. they do not have a personal, mature relationship with the Holy Spirit.[42] His point is that an ethnic Jew does not come into right relationship with God through mere outer ritual. Paul is not saying that ethnic Israel is eliminated from

God's plan or otherwise disqualified from His unconditional promises to that nation. This is made clear *in the very next passage:*

> "What advantage, then, is there in being a Jew, or what value is there in circumcision? Much in every way! [43] First of all, they have been entrusted with the very words of God. What if some did not have faith? Will their lack of faith nullify God's faithfulness? Not at all!" (Romans 3:1-4)

Galatians 3:28-29 further illustrates this point: "There is neither Jew nor Greek, slave nor free, male nor female, for you are all one in Christ Jesus."

Replacement proponents regard this as a key text indicating God no longer views the Jews as a distinct covenant people. To reach this conclusion, however, they must first dismiss the overall teaching of the Scriptures (as well as that of Paul, who authored the letter to the Galatians).

Secondly, replacement advocates do not properly consider the context of even this sentence. For who could reasonably deny that males and females continue to exist on the earth? Similarly, wherever the Old and New Testament Scriptures mention slavery, its existence is presupposed. (Today, those who would deny that distinctions in the work force exist[44] and are necessary should examine for themselves the results of the great socialist experiment in Russia.) With respect to the believer's standing before God and ability to partake in the blessings of salvation, these distinctions are irrelevant. But they are very relevant with respect to God's plans on earth.[45] Though we are all members of the one universal body of Christ, we are still individually distinct.

The above theological discussion is more than academic. Where the church of Jesus Christ has usurped all the blessings and promises to Israel, it has also ultimately helped lay justification for such notorious undertakings as the Crusades, the Spanish Inquisition, Hitler's "final solution," and now the tolerance of dangerous factions like Pamyat. This in mind, Jonathan and his colleagues tried as best they could to explain why they would not "understand" Pamyat's position: it is not one originating from the mind or heart of God, and it has caused untold harm to both the Jews and the church.[46]

39

Probably the Moscow journalist was the most pleased with the meeting that afternoon. There had been plenty of animated dialogue and not much agreement on anything. The talks had been cordial, however, and could possibly resume in the future. In any event, the journalist had an exclusive story. Jonathan and his two leaders, in the meantime, had only a couple of hours before the festival was scheduled to start . . .

It was not until several weeks later that we discovered, in the aftermath of Pamyat's withdrawn threats concerning the festival, an even more bizarre plot. An article appearing in a Russian newspaper the following month told of the arrest of a neofascist terrorist organization, "Legion Werewolf." The Werewolves apparently tried to burn down the stadium as the festival was taking place. Their plans were foiled, thankfully, by the Moscow police. According to the news article, Legion Werewolf "seeks the annihilation of democrats, Communists, national patriots and especially Jews."[47]

Notwithstanding Pamyat, Legion Werewolf, and a few angry Orthodox babushkee, still another acrimonious company of protesters convened in front of the stadium on opening night.

"Fellow Jews of Moscow, these foreigners are *meshumadim* (Yiddish for "apostates")! They are no longer Jews! They have destroyed themselves with Christianity, and now they are trying to destroy you with it!"

The commotion came from our ultra-Orthodox Jewish brothers with the long, black coats and side curls. Proudly calling themselves "anti-missionaries," some had flown in from Israel for the demonstration.

"Jesus is not for you!" they persisted, trying to turn their Jewish kinsmen away from the concert..

To most Western Jews, it is all right, maybe even good, for a Gentile to proselytize. But when a Jew tells others, especially other Jews, of God's love through Jesus, it is seen as treasonous. One simply cannot be both a Jew and a follower of Jesus, or so it is believed. If a Jew follows Jesus, therefore, he has *de facto* forsaken his God and his people. He is a traitor, a *meshumed*, to be shunned and despised, no matter what he says about his motives or his new faith. Some Jewish families will go so far as to hold mock funerals for their relatives who have become believers. From then on, the Messianic Jewish relative is considered dead. Any who relate to him defile themselves almost as if they'd dug up a corpse.

Like the Pharisees of Jesus' day, the anti-missionaries are highly zealous for the Talmudic[48] or rabbinic, as opposed to biblical, law and traditions. They trace their traditions back to the so-called *Hasidic* (Yiddish for "pious") rabbis of the post-Middle Ages. These pariah rabbis gained a following by embracing the ancient *Kabbalah*, esoteric Jewish mysticism of the sort strictly forbidden in the Old Testament.[49] Easily recognizable, members of these ultra-Orthodox sects like to dress in the same layered black garb as their forerunners in the Jewish ghettos of Eastern Europe 200 years ago.

The anti-missionaries' *raison d'être* is that Jesus is not now, never was, and never will be the Messiah. Their express purpose is to keep others in the fold from straying into faith in Him. They tail Jewish missionaries around the globe, seeking to undermine their every effort in the spread of the gospel. Unfortunately, they have been quite influential in Israel, inciting a good deal of persecution against Jewish believers there. Of them, Paul lamented:

"For I can testify about them that they are zealous for God, but their zeal is not based on knowledge…because they pursued [righteousness] not by faith but as if it were by works….As far as the gospel is concerned, they are enemies on your account; but as far as election is concerned, they are loved on account of the patriarchs, for God's gifts and His call are irrevocable." (Romans 10:2, 9:32, 11:28-29)

We look upon the anti-missionaries with love. Very few really know the Old Testament. Instead they have gotten inextricably entangled in the complicated writings of unregenerate rabbis. Jesus said to their predecessors long ago: "You diligently study the Scriptures because you think that by them you possess eternal life. These are the Scriptures that testify about Me, yet you refuse to come to Me to have life . . . Your accuser is Moses, on whom your hopes are set. If you believed Moses, you would believe Me, for he wrote about Me." (John 5: 39-40, 45-46) Yet Yeshua died for them, too. On rare occasion, we hear of an anti-missionary coming to faith. Inevitably he pays a tremendous price, losing just about everything he has in this life for the kingdom's sake.

All in all, we didn't mind the presence of the anti-missionaries so much at the festival. It was their attempt to keep others away from the stadium—and the truth—that we wouldn't tolerate. The Lord says: "Woe to you, teachers of the law and Pharisees. You hypocrites! You shut the kingdom of heaven in men's faces. You yourselves do not enter, nor will you let those enter who are trying to." (Matthew 23:13-14)

In the former Soviet Union, the ultra-Orthodox Jewish sects and therefore the anti-missionaries, are small in number and not highly esteemed. Nonetheless, they would not quit harassing our guests until forcibly driven off by the police. (Since then, the Messianic Jewish Festival has received the dubious distinction of uniting the anti-missionaries with the ultra-nationalists and neofascists, quite an unlikely coalition, all rallying for—or, rather, against—the same cause.)

✧   ✧   ✧   ✧

Moscow's Olympic Stadium, where the festival was held, is the largest indoor arena in Russia. Built for the 1980 Winter Olympics, it is much too large for most events and so has been split into two separate parts. Our group rented the half-stadium, with a seating capacity of about 17,000.

Poor Jonathan, I thought when I saw it for the first time, just before the concert. *This time he really* will *be preaching to empty chairs!*

The place was gargantuan. I was stupefied at its size. I'd been involved with Jewish ministry long enough to know it just didn't draw that much interest. Plus, I'd been out on the streets for the past week. I knew the Jews weren't exactly the most admired people group in the country. In fact, the forces set against our message were mind-boggling. What ever made us think multitudes would flock to a Messianic Jewish event, even if it were free?

My thoughts were interrupted by an armed security force suddenly emerging from side entrances and lining up all along the stage. Equipped with semi-automatic weapons dangling from their shoulders, the guardsmen posted themselves at carefully measured intervals. There they remained at attention for the entire concert. The sight was incredible! That ex-Soviet militia should now defend the rights of the Jews to preach the gospel was beyond my comprehension. My thoughts raced back once more to Bubby's stories. Instead of rounding us up for death as they had for centuries, these armed guards were actually helping us round people up for eternal life. Then I was reminded: "This is what the Lord says, He who made a way through the sea, a path through the mighty waters, who drew out the chariots and horses, the army and reinforcements together, and they lay there, never to rise again, extinguished, snuffed out like a wick: 'Forget the former things; do not dwell on the past. *See, I am doing a new thing*! Now it springs up; do you not perceive it?'" (Isaiah 43:18-19, emphasis added) Maybe the stadium wouldn't be too big after all. Who knew what the heavenly armies had been up to, and what forces and powers had been snuffed out to make way for the Lord and what He wanted to do?

It isn't always easy to forget the former things. From the day I gave my life to Jesus, and years before I ever heard of a Messianic Jewish movement, I'd longed to see the Jews embrace their Messiah. For "theirs is the adoption as sons; theirs the divine glory, the covenants, the receiving of the law, the temple worship and the promises. Theirs are the patriarchs, and from them is traced the human ancestry of Christ, who is God over all . . ." (Romans 11:4-5) But Western Jews have not yet been receptive for the most part. The call to Jewish ministry has therefore been mostly intercessory, sowing but not tangibly reaping, year in, year out. Of course, there has been some scattered fruit, and surrender to God's call, whatever that may be, has its own inherent reward. What greater prize can there be than acquaintance with the very heart of God, the kind found only in surrendered prayer?

According to the Scriptures, a spiritual hardness has come upon Israel until the full number of Gentiles comes into the kingdom of God. (Romans 11:25) By grace, God has reserved a remnant in Israel to be saved. (Romans 11:4-5) He has not rejected them as a nation. (Romans 11:1-2) He has also set a time for the hardness on them to be lifted. That date is related to the fulfillment of the times of the Gentiles. (Luke 21:24) As we approach the end of the age, God's gracious dealings with the nations will climax. (Luke 21:7-28) At that time His grace will dramatically turn again to Israel. Thus Jesus told His disciples: "Look at the fig tree (symbolic of Israel) and all the trees. When they sprout leaves, you can see for yourself and know that summer is near. Even so, when you see these things happening, you know that the kingdom of God is near." (Luke 21: 29-31) When the fig tree blossoms, when the Jewish people revive, the return of our King is at hand! Concerning those days, Jesus said, "Be always on the watch, and pray . . ." (Luke 21:36)

Meanwhile crowds streamed into Olympic Stadium. They came, Jew and Gentile alike, with all the cares and worries of a shared hard life. The unrelenting stresses and strains had led to rampant alcoholism, and we spotted not a few walking to their seats with bottle in hand. 'May they leave tonight filled with new wine, drunk in the joy of the Lord," we prayed.

The concert opened with joyful sounding notes of Hebraic praise. Colorfully costumed dancers worshipped the God of Israel. The audience clapped and nodded to the beat. Some even smiled—and quite expressively for a crowd of Muscovites. Soon it seemed the whole place was thawing from a sort of frozen stupor, coming to life before my eyes!

As the name of Yeshua was proclaimed and exalted, I knew something historic was happening. Centuries-old strongholds of anti-Semitism were being shattered, at least for a brief time. Ethnic hatreds and fears were melting under the warmth of Messiah's love. In addition, and not by human design, the festival was taking place during the Old Testament holiday of Shavuot, corresponding to Pentecost in the New Testament. Was this sheer coincidence—or did it underscore the Holy Spirit's doings?

I did not hear Jonathan's salvation message that evening. I was too engulfed in the moment, too caught up in the sense of God's imminent presence, too cognizant of the spiritual threshold we were crossing. Not normally prone to tears, I had turned into a veritable fountain. I had been touched by nothing less than God's joy at His Son's claiming His inheritance! "Ask of Me and I will make the nations Your inheritance," the Father says in Psalm 2:8. I had caught just a glimpse of the celebration taking place at that instant in the heavens—at the kingdom of God touching earth. For this joy, Jesus had endured the cross. I was witnessing the first fruits of the return of a prodigal nation and the Father's joyful welcome. It was a new thing.

Two thousand years ago, Jesus lamented over Israel: "O Jerusalem, Jerusalem, you who kill the prophets and stone those sent to you, how often I have longed to gather your children together, as a hen gathers her chicks under her wings, but you were not willing. Look, your house is left to you desolate. For I tell you, you will not see Me again until you say, 'Blessed is he who comes in the name of the Lord.'" (Matthew 23:37-39) At last, tonight, in Moscow, His people were running eagerly to His side! Yeshua's arms were still spread out wide, the little ones gathering gladly beneath His wings. Tonight they were saying, "Blessed is he who comes in the name of the Lord!" Tonight they would see Him again.

Moments later, Jonathan gave an altar call. Only a sprinkling of folks in the nearly-full stadium (other than the festival workers) did not stand to their feet to pray a sinner's prayer. We were stunned, our hearts pounding, our minds reeling with amazement.

According to festival organizers, 30,000 people attended the concerts over its three nights. (The organizers deliberately underestimate numbers to avoid exaggeration, since precise counts are impossible to obtain.). More than 10,000, they said, prayed to receive Yeshua. They estimated half of those to be Jewish, based on follow-up cards distributed at the concerts. In any case, such numbers of Jews coming to faith were indeed reminiscent of the Book of Acts. Pentecost was no coincidence.

With discipleship as a long-range goal, the ministry scheduled is first meeting of Moscow's brand new Messianic Jewish fellowship right on the heels of the concert. Thus Congregation *Shomer Yisrael* (Hebrew for "Israel's Watchman") came into existence the day after the festival. Drawing several hundred Russians to its first Shabbat service, it instantly became one of the largest Messianic congregational meetings in the world. In the midst of exuberant, near-delirious celebration, the fellowship's initial leadership team was ordained: a Messianic pastor from Chicago, the evangelist from

Maryland, and a young Jewish believer from Moscow.

The rejoicing went on and on and on. . ."He brought them out of darkness and the deepest gloom, and broke away their chains. Let them give thanks to the Lord for His unfailing love and His wonderful deeds for men!" (Psalm 107:14-15)

"Yes, we think this is true," Nikolai said. The wife and small daughter, neither of whom spoke any English, smiled as if they understood.

"I would like to ask you one thing," Chantal said. "When the concert is over, before you go home tonight, please try to find me. I know there are many people here, but God can help you find me."

Her smuggling operation successfully completed, Chantal headed out again, this time to talk to some of the anti-missionaries demonstrating against the festival in front of the concert hall. As always, they hoped to dissuade Jewish Belarussians from considering the claims of Christ. If she could get them chatting with her about one of their favorite topics of debate, such as the virgin birth, they would be distracted enough to leave the festival guests alone.

It wasn't hard to spot the black-garbed vigilantes or, since many of them spoke English, engage them in animated dialogue over rabbinical interpretations of Messianic prophecy. Chantal prayed under her breath as they talked. The conversation wasn't entirely pretext. After all, the Word of God never returns void!

The minutes passed quickly. Chantal had to extricate herself and get back inside before the concert began. "I encourage you not to rely on the rabbis but to read the Scriptures for yourselves," she said. "God will speak to you when you read the Bible. It will be different from reading the commentaries and interpretations. Please try it."

Chantal turned and walked back around the crowd, toward the barricade gates in front of the glass doors. But something didn't look right. From a hundred or so feet away, she could see the doors were closing, inch by inch. The police had abandoned their barricade posts and gone inside. They appeared to be using their full weight to pull the doors shut. The crowd kept pushing; some clung with their fingers to the door jamb. Furtively trying to slip in, they came close to getting crushed. There was mass confusion and tumult. Chantal pushed hard against the others and made it up to the door, but not in time. She was locked out.

Pressed up against the glass and nervously waving her arms, she could at least tell that her team members indoors noticed her. But dozens of people continued to push hard all around her. If a door were opened to let her in, they might not be able to close it again. Chantal began to panic. *I could die out here*, she thought. *I could get pushed through* *the glass or stomped to death. I can't even speak Russian. . .*Then she felt a wave of peace. *. .No, God wouldn't have brought me here to get crushed to death. "I will not fear the tens of thousands drawn up against me on every side!"* (Psalms 3:6)

One of the workers inside held up a large sign in English, telling her to go to the back door. For a moment it seemed a way had been made. She wriggled out from the bodies pressing against her. But alas, by the time she reached the back door, a throng was already there to greet her. Some English-speaking Belarussians had apparently also read the sign and now they, too, expected to get in. In any event, the workers inside had neglected to inform the dutiful Russian security guards at the back door of the plan. Since she didn't have advance security clearance, they wouldn't let her, or anyone else, get one step past them.

Disheartened, Chantal turned and started at the crowd pressing in around her. Like most other first-time missionaries from the West, she'd never before witnessed such widespread spiritual hunger, such desperation for truth and hope. *Like sheep without a shepherd*, she thought. All ages surrounded her: young children whose hands parents held tightly in theirs; teenagers with cigarettes dangling out of the corners of their mouths; fatigued factory and office workers; weather-beaten, bent-over senior citizens. Many were extremely dressed-up by American standards, as if all decked out for a night at the theater. A good number of the older men proudly displayed war medals on their coat jackets. A few in the crowd looked impoverished. But there was one thing they all had in common: hungering eyes.

Chantal thought of the crowds that pressed in on Yeshua and His response to them: "Seeing the multitudes, He was moved with com-passion...." A tear trickled down her flustered cheek. When the disciples wanted to send the multitudes away, Jesus wanted them to stay and be fed—with whatever little the twelve had on hand. Despite the ministry and need for workers indoors, she knew God wanted her outside. "Those who had been scattered preached the Word wherever they went." (Acts 8:4)

"I should be in there," came a dejected-sounding voice from nearby. "I thought maybe I could have helped because I speak English and I am a believer."

Chantal was startled only for a second or two. She turned quickly in the direction of the voice and found a young Belarussian woman standing to her left. "No, I think you should be right here!" she answered. "If you will translate for me, we can minister to some of these people who could not get in. This, I think, is what the Lord would do."

The young woman looked out at the crowd. Her face lit up. "Yes, I can see you will need me," she said, extending her right hand. "My name is Natasha."

The two walked back around to the front of the concert hall. The crowd was still gathered, though the festival was well underway. Since Chantal wore an official ministry badge, dozens of people instantly approached her with questions. Among them was the President of the local Holocaust survivors group, as well as the Belarussian national TV network crew that had planned to film the concert that night.

Chantal tried to be gracious to these disappointed guests. "We're so sorry this happened," she said, via her new-found translator. "We had no idea so many people would come. But the same message that will be given inside I can tell you out here. All the songs that will be sung are about the love of God for all people. God loved the world so much that He sent us His Son, Yeshua the Messiah, for both Jews and non-Jews. Through Him, all our sins can be forgiven and we can have peace with God."

Chantal continued, noticing that, as time went on, she was no longer talking to just a handful of people. A small crowd had encircled her and Natasha. Normally she disliked speaking in public—and certainly would never have thought of herself as a preacher.

"Would any of you like to commit your lives to Yeshua?" she asked a few minutes later. Chantal's heart pounded while she watched several heads nod and hands raise. *When God shuts one door, He really does open another!* she thought.

The evening hours flew by for the ad hoc pair of evangelists. They would preach to one group, lead them in a sinner's prayer of repentance, urge them to connect to a local church, and then start all over with another little flock of curious faces. Eventually, as it grew late, the guests inside began trickling out of the concert hall. Suddenly Nikolai and his family reappeared, their faces aglow.

They greeted Chantal with three wide smiles. "Thank you for letting us in. It was just as you said! Much more than a concert! We all asked Jesus to come into our hearts tonight! We have very much to think about now."

Nikolai threw his head back and upward toward heaven, revealing a radiant mouthful of large gold crowns capping his teeth. He waved his arms exuberantly at the sky. "Our lives will be very different now." He kissed Chantal's hand again as his wife kissed her cheek. "We only wish you would not leave Minsk."

✧   ✧   ✧   ✧

The Belarussians' ardent embrace of the Savior was especially glorious in view of the upheaval and governmental opposition the festival had unwittingly generated just days earlier.

In the early morning, the day before the festival was to begin, Jonathan received an urgent phone call from the local church serving as the festival's official sponsor (As in other former Soviet republics, foreign missionary activities in Belarus were permitted only if sponsored by a state-registered church.) The government wanted to cancel the festival, they told Jonathan, due to last-minute pressure from the Israeli Embassy. They were afraid, they actually said, that war might break out amongst the Jews of Belarus. We could go forward with the concert but it could not be a "religious" event. In the meantime, we were to stop all street evangelism and leafleting, as well as festival advertising, immediately.

We were stunned. Up until now, everything had gone so well. The outreach work force from North America, Western Europe, Israel and Russia had blended together beautifully. The Belarussian media had been interested in the festival and cooperative. The people of Minsk had been warm and receptive. The Lord had been faithful to either smooth out the usual bumps in the road or detour us around them. We had delighted in His goodness. Could this roadblock have come from Him or was it the doing of an adversary?

The sponsoring church had little information and the officials were not interested in discussing the matter with "foreigners." Festival leaders decided to send their own director of security, a Russian gentleman who'd lived for a time in Belarus, to talk with government officials downtown. Alex could be wise as a serpent but harmless as a dove. Festival organizers knew he could be entrusted with sensitive political matters.

In the meantime, all the other outreach workers were summoned to a corporate prayer meeting. After the troops assembled, the news was announced. A solemn hush descended on the group. Then the technical/staging director sprang to his feet. "Last night when we were praying for Jonathan," Bruce said, "a portion of Nehemiah 2:10 kept coming to me: 'There had come a man to seek the welfare of the children of Israel.' (KJV) This morning, during my devotions, I turned to this Scripture to pray again for Jonathan. That's when I saw the first part of this verse. It said, '*The governors were angry* that there had come a man to seek the welfare of the children of Israel.' I thought, 'But God, we've had good favor with the government here.' Nonetheless, God was moving me to pray for this."

"God isn't taken by surprise as we have been this morning. We must be encouraged. The result of the fight against Nehemiah was that the opposing governors did not win and the city of Jerusalem was rebuilt. The government doesn't stand a chance against God's purposes!"

Exuberant applause and shouts of praise exploded in the room. Carol, our director of intercession, was next to speak. "Before the outreach began, the Lord impressed on me that we would see the power of the blood of Jesus to impact a nation, not just a city, through this festival. He spoke to me through II Chronicles 13. In that chapter, Israel had come against Judah in battle. Judah's response was that they had priests who ministered to the Lord day and night and that He was fighting for them. Our "priests," the intercessors, have not forsaken the Lord and they have ministered to Him day and night. His Word says He will fight for us!"

Another wave of praise rippled across the assembly. It was not an easily intimidated or discouraged group.

Carol continued. "Second Chronicles 13 says the priests sounded the trumpet and God delivered into Judah's hand those who had come against them. Under the New Covenant, when people are delivered into our hands, it means they get saved!

"Hallelujah, Lord! Your priests sound the trumpet and shout to You for the victory in this battle! By Your hand, deliver the people into our hands! Save the people of this city – and of this nation!"

The whole team prayed: "Why do the nations conspire and the peoples plot in vain? The kings of the earth take their stand and the rulers gather together against the Lord and against His Anointed One. 'Let us break their chains,' they say, 'and throw off their fetters.' The One enthroned in heaven laughs; the Lord scoffs at them. Then He rebukes them in His anger and terrifies them in His wrath, saying, 'I have installed my King on Zion, My holy hill.'"

"I will proclaim the decree of the Lord: He said to Me, 'You are My Son; today I have become your Father. Ask of Me and I will make the nations Your inheritance, the ends of the earth Your possession!'" (Psalm 2:1-8)

Jonathan took the floor next to lay out a revised strategy. He faced an army geared up to fight. "We do not believe God's opposers will succeed. The Israeli Embassy, anti-missionaries and Orthodox Jews will not keep the gospel from reaching the Jewish people here!

"Although the government would like to cancel the festival outright, they said they would give us a trial run tomorrow night. They said we could go forward with the concert strictly as a cultural event. They will have officials there to monitor us. They warned us they will shut the festival down if we preach. But as I was praying, the Lord showed me I could still explain the songs. Not only I, but the singers as well, could testify about the biblical and Jewish reality behind the music. So I will be sharing about the Jewishness of the message of the cross in all the songs and inviting the people to pray with me at the end!

"We were also told to stop all festival advertising and street evangelism, but we've already run plenty of ads in the papers, as well as on TV and radio. We've plastered posters all over the city. So we will release the evangelists this afternoon to go out in the streets and prayerwalk instead of pass out leaflets. Prayer is our primary weapon in this battle. And, outreach team members, if anyone asks what you're doing, you still have the constitutional freedom of speech in this country to talk and pray with them.

"Then, after the first night of the festival, instead of continuing with street work, the evangelists will begin the work of discipleship. We're going to ask the Lord for divine appointments at the concert and then arrange follow-up visits with those who make professions of faith. Don't be afraid or discouraged; the battle belongs to the Lord!"

Jonathan stepped down amidst the cheering, while one of the team leaders led in more prayer:

". . .'Sovereign Lord. . .You made the heaven and the earth and the sea and everything in them. You spoke by the Holy Spirit through the mouth of your servant, our father David; 'Why do the nations rage and the peoples plot in vain? The kings of the earth take their stand and the rulers gather together against the Lord and against His Anointed One.' Indeed Herod and Pontius Pilate met together with the Gentiles and the people of Israel in this city to conspire against your holy servant, Jesus, whom You anointed. They did what your power and will had decided beforehand should happen. *Now, Lord, consider their threats and enable Your servants to speak Your word with great boldness.* Stretch out Your hand to heal and perform miraculous signs and wonders through the name of Your holy servant, Jesus.'" (Acts 4:24-30, emphasis added)

The Lord strengthened us with expectant faith as we prayed. The opposition only gave Him greater opportunity to prove Himself strong! We knew the real battle was not against flesh and blood, nor against any man, organization or government. As the prayer meeting drew to an optimistic close, a final word resounded prophetically, "The king's heart is in the hand of the Lord; He directs it like a watercourse wherever He pleases." (Proverbs 21:1). . .

When Alex returned from his conclave with the officials downtown, however, he did not bring good news. The roadblock, he said, was the Belarussian Committee for Religious Affairs, comprised in its entirety of two women. Based on "warnings" from the Israeli Embassy, the Committee feared the festival could result in civil war among the Jews. As a result the concert could not go on as a religious program. Allowance would be made to present it as a cultural exchange because our official documents described it as an "international Christian festival of Jewish song and dance." But the Committee insisted there be no preaching and only a very short time of prayer. The two women assured Alex they would be at the festival on the first night to monitor compliance with their demands. They threatened to take action against the church sponsoring the festival, as well as deport Jonathan from Belarus, if we tried to appeal or protest against their decision.

No legal recourse of any kind was available to us, Alex said. The judicial system was far too grid-locked to address our concerns. Apparently, the state had the power, if not the technical right, to do whatever it wished with us. "You must remember," Alex said, "all they have known their whole lives until recently is Communism. People don't change overnight."

Sometimes, in fact, things don't change over centuries. Unsaved rabbinic Jews with political pull have continued to stir up strife against Jewish believers since Yeshua and His disciples walked the earth. We faced a modern-day reenactment of Acts 14:2: "The Jews who refused to believe stirred up the Gentiles and poisoned their minds against the brothers." The local sponsoring church in Minsk had chosen courageously to align with their Messianic brethren in the faith. The congregation's love for Israel was sincere. They were willing to risk the loss of good will with the unsaved Jewish community and local Orthodox church to stand with fellow members of the household of faith. Though small in number, the church was big in heart. How could we, in turn, do anything to antagonize the government against them?

Festival leaders beseeched the Lord for wisdom. At the same time, the intercessors relentlessly cried out for mercy and victory. The administrators ironed out details for alternate scenarios that might unfold. Meanwhile, the evangelists stepped into a divine rerouting of surprise and blessing—especially the team led by Chantal's husband, Stewart.

Stewart brimmed with expectation at the sudden turn of events. Since the previous evening, a particular passage from the Book of Acts had been percolating in his mind.

"Paul and his companions traveled throughout the region of Phrygia and Galatia, *having been kept by the Holy Spirit from preaching the Word* in the province of Asia. When they came to the border of Mysia, they tried to enter Bithynia but the Spirit of Jesus would not allow them to. So they passed by Mysia and went down to Troas. During the night, Paul had a vision of a man of Macedonia standing and begging him, 'Come over to Macedonia and help us.' After Paul had seen the vision, we got ready at once to leave for Macedonia, concluding that God had called us to preach the gospel to them." (Acts 16:6-10, emphasis added)

Stewart was certain that God had many "Macedonians" who would not be at the festival but needed and wanted help. This morning's abrupt change of direction undoubtedly meant that "God had called us to preach the gospel to them." Surely He would be faithful to show us who and where they were!

Stewart's enthusiasm was contagious and spread to the rest of his team of Americans and ex-Soviets. One of the Belarussians ventured an idea. "I know a Christian doctor who is the assistant director of a children's hospital here," she said. "Maybe he will allow us to visit the children and minister to them."

Stewart immediately liked the suggestion. A short phone call and Metro ride later, he and the team found themselves welcomed into the hospital. The assistant director and staff, outfitted in white coats and tall, chef-like white hats, were warm and gracious.

The Americans tried to hide their shock and dismay at the sight of the hospital. It was the first any of them had seen of the typically ill-supplied, sorely outmoded, Soviet-era medical facilities nobly struggling to stay semi-operative. The hospital had no money for upkeep; dirt and grime were everywhere. A putrid odor filled the corridors. Arcane equipment, supplies and furniture, circa World War II in style and appearance, lay broken in pieces in patients' rooms, laboratories and offices. Hospital beds were filled with children suffering from everything from the flu to the dreadful effects of the Chernobyl disaster. *How*, Stewart wondered, *could any of them get well in a place like this?*

The team split into small groups and went from room to room, greeting the children with big smiles and hugs, singing and praying for them, and sharing Jesus' love. On one floor, most of the children were well enough to gather in the waiting room. So a translator improvised an animated play for them about a good sea captain named Jesus who saved his crew from shipwreck.

By the end of the afternoon, many of the delighted little patients asked the Lord into their hearts. Gospel tracts and festival invitations were given to the staff and visiting parents, who were almost as eager to be prayed for as the children.

Many tears, hugs and prayers later, the team said their bittersweet good-byes. The place had indeed been their Macedonia for the day. Stewart was elated, despite the pummeling his heart had taken from witnessing such pain and privation. But the children's faces would not fade from his mind. *Come back to Macedonia and help us*, they echoed relentlessly.

The hospital ministry seemed so divinely ordered that the next day several teams, equipped with translators and musicians, visited different hospitals all around the city. Minsk, we quickly learned, was a city replete with disease. Malnutrition, alcoholism and industrial pollution had taken their toll throughout the former Soviet Union. But in addition, Minsk (actually, the whole republic of Belarus) has, for over a decade, suffered the brunt of the world's worst-ever environmental disaster.

The Chernobyl explosion of 1986 occurred several hundred miles south of Belarus in northern Ukraine. The direction and force of the winds that day, however, haplessly landed seventy percent of the radioactive fallout onto Belarus.[50] There, it instantly and without warming contaminated the region's air, water, food chain, and animal and human populations. Over two million Belarussians were suffering some form of radiation sickness at the time of our visit.[51] Most sensitive to the radiation were, and still are, the children. The childhood cancer rate remains high, even for those youngsters born years after the accident.

A deadly toll was also exacted from the Soviet workers employed at the facility. We had the unexpected opportunity to meet and talk briefly with a few of them. These men would not share in depth, they said, because they didn't want to make us sad. They did disclose that over a hundred Chernobyl clean-up workers were living in Minsk. All were terminally ill. They received no special compensation or medical assistance from the government.

The men we met had been sent in to cap the blown reactor. As they worked, they said, they developed a slight headache and a sweet taste in their mouths. They knew the risk of contamination was high but were not told anything specific about it until well after the assignment. Then they got sick.

It was hard to detect bitterness or resentment among these courageous and humble men. They felt they had simply done what was necessary. The general population of Belarus, on the other hand, seemed much angrier over the incident.[52] The Soviet government, they felt, could and should have prevented the accident but failed to heed obvious warnings or take reasonable precautions. Especially distressing to them was that they were not made aware of the explosion when it occurred, or warned that most of the radiation was falling out on them.

The name "Chernobyl" mean "darkness" or "blackness." To the Belarussians, that is precisely what fell out of the sky in 1986. But ten years later they were seeing a great light. The victimized people of Minsk knew they needed help—and that it could come only from heaven above.

✧ ✧ ✧ ✧

Thus the crowds flocked in droves to the Messianic gospel concert, shocking everyone who had planned the event. *If Nikolai and his family are any indication, God worked wonders inside that hall tonight,* Chantal thought as she embraced her beaming and affectionate new friends.

"We wish you would not leave Minsk," Nikolai repeated. "We have very much to learn now about God and the Bible."

"There are many good churches in this city eager to help you," Chantal answered. She pointed to a list of them printed in the program that Nadia, Nikolai's wife, still held. "Perhaps eventually a Messianic Jewish congregation will start from the festival."

Nikolai translated for Nadia. She smiled and nodded. "That we would really like," he said wistfully.

There were more hugs and kisses but Chantal had to go and find her husband. Stewart would certainly be worried about her having been locked outdoors all evening, and she was anxious to learn what had happened indoors in the meantime. Had Jonathan found a way to preach the gospel? Had many people responded? What about the women from the Religious Affairs Committee? Would there be another festival tomorrow night?

Chantal and Stewart met in the lobby. Each could quickly tell from the other's face that all had gone well. Each was bubbling with a testimony of God's victorious power. "Yeshua had His Macedonians for you tonight," Stewart said, relieved when he heard how the Lord had directed his wife's steps.

The whole evening, it turned out, bore the fingerprints of He Who pieces all things together for His glory. As for the Religious Affairs Committee, Alex had offered them special passes for reserved seats and concert hall access through the back door the day before. They had declined, saying they had their own connections. The "connections," however, proved no match for the unwieldy masses surrounding the building. As a result, and to their consternation, the two religious monitors ended up lost in the crowd and locked out of the stadium the entire evening. In the meantime, unaware of their plight, Jonathan took the opportunity to thank them from the stage for permitting the festival to go on. In response, a grateful audience cheered and applauded their beneficent Committee. "God bless you, ladies, tonight, and your whole city," Jonathan said, as the frustrated pair paced outside from door to door.

"We have not come here to preach," Jonathan had made clear at the outset, "but to share with you in song and dance the peace and joy that can be found by anyone, anywhere, in a personal relationship with the God of Israel. Our culture, our songs and dances, all center around our God. We hope you are blessed in the cultural exchange tonight and enjoy God's presence."

As the music began, Hebraic-style dancers ran down the aisles to the front of the stage. The dance team had been resourceful. Only the day before, when Alex returned from his meeting with the Religious Committee, did we learn that official papers identified the festival as a *cultural* exchange of song *and dance*. We had no choice; some kind of Israeli folk-style dance group would have to be put, or rather thrown, together. With little over twenty-four hours' notice, a good-natured intercessor agreed to recruit a team and coordinate some steps. The dancers would have to do without costumes. Nobody had brought any and there was no place to buy them in Minsk. They would also have to do without much practice. Basically, their hope and prayer was that enough people would join in that the amateur-level performance would not be noticed for very long.

It was obvious the Lord was with the dancers. Anointing and multiplying what little they had to offer, He made it enough to feed the many. A sweet spirit of celebration was released when these "non-troupe troopers" worshipped before Him. Countless others joined in, and His radiant joy consumed the place..

Two of the festival singers from Europe were well known to the Belarussians. Victor Klimenko of Finland and Helen Shapiro of Great Britain had each enjoyed substantial renown in Europe before dedicating their lives to the Lord. The audience loved their music and listened carefully as they explained their songs about God's love and salvation. Naturally Victor and Helen also explained how their lives and careers had changed as a result of embracing Messiah. At the word of their testimony, thousands of faces were transfixed in a silence that shouted. Jonathan heard it. He felt the Holy Spirit's nudging: "Then they [the Jewish rulers] called [them] in again and commanded them not to speak or teach at all in the name of Jesus. But [they] replied, 'Judge for yourselves whether it is right in God's sight to obey you rather than God. For we cannot help speaking about what we have seen and heard.'" (Acts 4:18-20). Jonathan couldn't let the opportunity slip by. He walked back on stage.

"Tonight, the singers and I have told you about God's free gift of eternal life in His Son, Jesus, or Yeshua. If you would like to ask God to forgive you of your sins and have never done that before, I invite you to stand up right now, where you're seated – but do this only if you are willing to live for Him the rest of your life."

Jonathan watched at least two-thirds of the audience rise to their feet. He knew he'd have to choose his next words carefully. "I will pray a simple prayer aloud to God. If those of you who are standing will repeat what I say, silently, in your hearts, God will hear you. Your life will be changed forever."

The outreach team held their breath and prayed, half rejoicing at the victory of the moment, half wondering if they would be on the next flight out of Belarus. They jumped from their seats when Jonathan instructed those who had just given their lives to Christ to go to the lobby and look for workers with badges so follow-up could begin.

Some government officials and dignitaries, we later learned, had made it into the concert hall that night. Others, including the Minister of Culture, were locked out, along with the Religious Affairs Committee and the TV crew. Most of the reporters and other media representatives who came got in and, by the next day, the festival was news all over the city. The articles and news reports were astonishingly favorable.

Some of the impact could probably be explained by the fact that Minsk was a less cosmopolitan city than Moscow or St. Petersburg. The performing arts were relatively rare. A festival from abroad offered free of charge was practically unheard of. But we knew it was the Lord who had masterminded the miraculous.

"His purpose was to create in Himself one new man out of the two [Jew and Gentile], thus making peace and, in this one body, to reconcile both of them to God through the cross, by which He put to death their hostility." (Ephesians 2:15-16) The press, as well as the politicians, had seized on the same theme: Jesus is the Savior of all— of the Jew, Belarussian, and Russian. The God who loves us all has made it possible for us to love one another in Christ. The festival offered a welcome word of peace, the newsmen said. The politicians commented on the hope that had been extended to their troubled and ethnically divisive country.

Meanwhile, those from whom we'd expected opposition were strangely silent. Several Holocaust survivors had come that first night and stood for the sinner's prayer. The concert hall director voiced no complaints other than the need for better crowd control. The Orthodox Jews and Israeli Ambassador were too offended to attend, so they apparently lodged no specific complaints either. In the wake of such a reception, how could the Religious Committee cancel the festival?

Our corporate prayer meeting that day was filled with awe and thanksgiving. We echoed the psalmist's victory cry:

"In my distress I called to the Lord; I cried to my God for help . . . He shot His arrows and scattered the enemies . . . He rescued me from my powerful enemy, from my foes, who were too strong for me . . . To the faithful you show yourself faithful, to the blameless, you show yourself blameless, to the pure you show yourself pure, but to the crooked, you show yourself shrewd. You save the humble but bring low those whose eyes are haughty . . . With your help I can advance against a troop; with my God I can scale a wall. As for God, His way is perfect. . .He trains my hands for battle; my arms can bend a bow of bronze. You give me Your shield of victory, and Your right hand sustains me . . . You made my enemies turn their backs in flight . . . Praise be to my Rock! Exalted be God my Savior!" (Psalm 18)

The next night, evangelism teams were assigned to minister to the overflow crowds outside the concert hall. Those who could play a musical instrument found themselves outside, leading worship under the stars. All the while, intercessors roved the area, covering the ground in prayer.

Predictably, several thousand people gathered early for the second night, pushing and pressing again in all directions. The police were soon exasperated with what threatened to be a repeat of the previous evening's ordeal. As a result, and in contrast to the night before, they happily handed over their megaphones and makeshift platform to one of the festival leaders. David's words of welcome and comfort spoken to the crowd were instantly calming. As the hungry multitudes were assured they would all get fed one way or another, inside or out, furtive desperation gave way to peaceable order. From then on, the police were content to serve merely as ushers. (By the third night, the crowd actually became tranquil, politely forming a snake-like cue spanning the distance from the concert hall to the Metro stop about 2,000 feet away.)

Stewart was elated to be among those appointed to preach out-doors. It had been a long time since he'd done anything remotely like this. He had no time either to think of a message or be too nervous about not having one. He only knew that whenever he looked into the eyes of the beautiful but beaten-down people of Minsk, "springs of water welling up to eternal life" came from deep inside. It was a new, almost giddying experience, this flow of the Spirit.

The wells of salvation were plentiful that night. He, like the others preaching outdoors, watched many begin to drink of the rivers of living water. One of those was a Jewish woman named Sofia.

Sofia was determined to prepare a home-cooked meal for the foreigners who had come so far and ministered to her. She printed her name and phone number on a crumpled-up piece of paper. Then, at the end of the evening, she placed it carefully in Stewart's hand, on top of a pile of similar little scraps. "Please come to my apartment for dinner before you leave Minsk," she said. "I really must talk more with you."

Stewart woke up the next morning to a mental picture of Sofia's face, her eyes still beckoning. Thinking again of Paul and the Macedonians, he phoned the number on the ragged little paper with her name on it. "My wife and I would like to accept your invitation and visit you today," he said. Sofia was elated.

Sofia's home was a typical, Soviet-style Minsk flat. Though primitive and small, it was scrubbed clean and tidy. Its eclectic array of furnishings appeared to have been handed down for generations. Sofia had lived the kind of tragic life that was also rather typically Soviet. Her son had died in a car accident while in his early 20's, a few months before he was to have been married. As a result, Sofia sank into a prolonged depression which, in turn, caused her husband to divorce her. She was just beginning to feel better and was planning to make aliyah with her sister when the sister died suddenly a few months ago. Sofia, an English teacher, still hoped to emigrate to Israel by the end of the year—if she could find the strength to go on with life at all.[53]

Sofia had not yet given her life to the Lord. "I am trying now to learn what is the truth and to understand what it means to be a Jew," she said. "For most of my life, under Communism, this was not possible. So now I try to see if there is God and, if there is, why He makes us suffer so much." She sighed and trembled slightly. "I understand what you spoke about last night but I still do not understand why there is so much suffering in life."

Stewart and Chantal shared from the Scriptures about God's love and compassion, mercy and forgiveness, judgment and justice. They listened and responded to question upon question. Obviously, Sofia had been soul-and-spirit searching for a long time. Nonetheless, she had a soft heart that melted like snow at the rising of the sun. At last, she said hours later, she knew there was a purpose for going on with her life. She wanted to serve her Messiah.

Together they prayed and wept. There was too little time before the couple had to leave. Only the most rudimentary follow-up counsel could be given. Sofia didn't have a Bible, but since she spoke English, Stewart and Chantal left her theirs—along with a piece of their hearts. "Someday soon, this Bible will be read in Israel to other Jews from the CIS," Sofia assured them.

They didn't know it then, but someday soon Stewart, Chantal and their children would move to Minsk to pastor a Messianic congregation formed from the festival. From this group, churches throughout Belarus would be touched in years to come by the vision of the restoration of the Jews. . .

✧　✧　✧　✧

If Sofia, in the meantime, had stolen a bit of Stewart and Chantal's hearts, it was Felix, the president of the local Holocaust survivors association, who sliced a sizable chunk out of us all.

Felix was a gentle man whose sad eyes betrayed his eager smile. A secular Jew (i.e., not religiously observant) and a journalist, he was only three years old when World War II broke out. But he remembers it well. The Nazis, he said, cordoned off a whole portion of Minsk and converted it into a ghetto camp for the extermination of Jews. The atrocities committed there were hidden from much of the world until the collapse of the Soviet Union. The ghetto site just happened to be a short walk from our hotel. Felix offered to give us a personal tour, along with an historical account of the Minsk Ghetto. Our entire group was interested.

Our tour took place under an appropriately ashen gray, drizzling sky. Our first stop, just a couple of blocks from the hotel, was at a dark, obelisk-like monument at the bottom of a large dugout in a small park. Inscriptions in both Russian and Hebrew memorialized the slaughter at this site of 5,000 Jews on the holiday of Purim in March 1942.[54]

Purim is the celebration of God's miraculous preservation of the Jewish people recounted in the Book of Esther. It commemorates Haman's unsuccessful attempt to annihilate the Jews living in the Persian Empire nearly 2,500 years ago. The Nazis' selection of Purim as the execution date was deliberate. They wanted to show that, this time, there would be no miracle.[55]

On the morning of March 2, the Nazis ordered Jewish foremen, each of whom were compelled to help administrate the ghetto, to gather 5,000 women and children. The foremen refused, some losing their lives as a result. So the soldiers themselves promptly rounded up the victims, emptying the entire population of the ghetto orphanage, together with the orphans' teacher and doctor, to meet their quota. By nightfall, all 5,000 were machine gunned and buried en masse in a large pit, some of them while they were still alive.[56]

But the bloodiest of the pogroms, Felix said, took place over a three-day period in July of the same year,[57] following a heavy rainfall. Thousands upon thousands of Jews were brutally and systematically slaughtered. Their blood, mixed with rain water, swept through the streets of the city. Some of the prisoners were made to dig ditches but these were useless to stem the grotesque overflow. Eventually, the reddened flood waters washed into the river running through Minsk, saturating the summer air with its sickening bloody steam. When the carnage finally came to an end, an estimated 30,000 had been slain.

The horrors began, Felix said, when the Nazis captured Minsk in June 1941, six days after the war began. Within a few weeks, they divided Belarus into thirds and demanded the registration of every Jew in the country. All the Jews registered in one section were herded into concentration camps. Those in another part, which included Minsk, were confined to ghettos. The Jews in the remaining third of the country suffered the least; they were instantly shot and killed. Approximately 100,000 Jews, many of whom were brought in from other Nazi-occupied countries,[58] were destined for the Minsk Ghetto. Of these, only about 4,500, including Felix, survived the war.[59]

Felix was confined to the ghetto with his mother in August 1941. There, she helped organize a special underground resistance group to accommodate women, children and the elderly. (Although one of the best Jewish underground war networks existed in Minsk,[60] generally only able-bodied adult men were accepted in it.) This group's priority was its children, for whom it set up fake identity papers and a small school. Using bark from birch trees, Felix and his "classmates" learned how to read, write—and survive. Two years later, when the ghetto was liquidated by Nazi troops (assisted by Belarussians and Russians), it was the resistance group that got him out.

Felix spoke much about starvation during the war. Most of the ghetto inhabitants who weren't shot or gassed died from starvation, he said. Once, shortly after the ghetto was liquidated, he remembered that his mother had wrapped a gold watch in a white cloth and tossed it in the snow. He managed to find the watch and sell it so he could buy food. All the survivors (there were about 225 living in Minsk in 1994) still ate very quickly, he said. They were careful never to leave any scraps of food on their plates. Sadly, they all suffered from gastrointestinal problems and heart disease. Feelings of starvation still haunted Felix, he said, even when he knew he had plenty to eat.

It was hard for Felix to talk about the terror of the past but it would be even harder, he said, not to talk. Because there were so few survivors of the Minsk Ghetto, relatively little is known about what happened in his city. What is known must be voiced; too many had been silenced forever. As it is, he said, already the vast majority of young people in Minsk don't know the ghetto ever existed.

Soberly, we walked a few more blocks toward the central part of the ghetto, down a residential street preserved practically intact since the war. Shuffling as a group past these uninhabited, dilapidated wooden cottages with metal roofs and unkempt yards, we thought of the countless other, much more horrified groups that had preceded us down the same path—never to return. We thought of the Jewish Christians who must have been among them.[61]

Tall, trunk-twisted trees stood the full length of this timeworn street. In some odd manner, they beckoned to us, as if they too had a story to tell. Like Felix, they couldn't be silenced; every rustle of their leaves seemed a whispered lament, a grievous testimony of human history.

The Bible speaks of the testimony of creation. It even records an instance where Joshua set a rock under a tree to be a witness against the children of Israel. The rock, he said, "has heard all the words of the Lord which He spoke to us...." (Joshua 24:27, NAS) The Scriptures say that "the trees of the forest will sing for joy" (Psalm 96:12) and "clap their hands" (Isaiah 55:12), but now they "groan" for redemption (Romans 8:19-22). Who knows who hears the plaintive witness of the trees bordering the Minsk Ghetto?

Felix's tour included another few plaques on buildings and monuments. The most notable was erected in 1993 by the citizens of Hamburg, Germany, in memory of the 1,300 Hamburg Jews killed in the Minsk Ghetto. Notable too was that 24-hour police protection was needed to guard the monument against vandalism when it was put in place.

It was alongside the Hamburg Memorial that our group gathered to pray the *Kaddish* (traditional Jewish mourners' prayer). The Kaddish makes no mention of the dead. Instead, it asserts the greatness of God who works good from evil and will ultimately achieve perfect justice. We recited the Kaddish and mourned for those of our people who had perished here with no hope of salvation. At the same time, we thanked God for the privilege of praying on ground the devil had deemed for himself fifty years ago.

Felix's tour gave us a better idea of the depth of the wounds of ethnic hatred and fear in Belarus. The "putting to death of hostility between Jews and Gentiles" in such a place would be no simple feat. There was, in fact, much need in Belarus for the putting to death of hostility between Gentile and Gentile. Historical conflicts between Belarus and its neighbors had left the different nationalities in the country still at odds. But all the more opportunity for the Lord to work . . .

It should not have shocked us therefore, when, toward the end of the week, the concert hall director asked us to extend the festival. Too many people had been locked out and turned away each night, he said. The controversy with the Religious Affairs Committee had only resulted in more publicity, which had drawn out even larger crowds. The political dignitaries who'd come said they felt the festival's message was good for the city and the country. Naturally all of this was good for the concert hall. So, he asked, would we please consider staying one more night?

"Why do the nations conspire and the peoples plot in vain? . . . The One enthroned in heaven laughs . . ." (Psalm 2:1,4) We laughed as well. A couple of days before, we wouldn't have believed it. We rejoiced not in the approval of men but in their change of heart toward the Lord. The festival leaders unanimously agreed to put on an extra concert. But there remained, despite everyone's good intentions, the matter of the Religious Affairs Committee. We would have to go and get their permission all over again.

The next morning, Alex was back downtown at the Religious Affairs office, together with David, neither of them knowing what to expect.

Alex tried to be respectful. "The concert hall director, as you may know, has asked us to extend the festival one more night. Of course, we need your permission to do this."

"This festival is the biggest celebration ever held in Minsk," said one of the two committeewomen. "It is drawing people from all over Belarus and bringing them into the city. Of course, this is good for our city . . . and we have been instructed to cooperate with you."

Alex and David stared wide-eyed at each other.

"I do have a question," said the other woman, looking a little confused. "I myself am half Jewish, but I am unable to understand the difference between what you call Messianic Judaism and Orthodox Judaism. Also I have information from another Jewish group that I do not understand." She pointed to an anti-missionary leaflet, lying on her desk. "Can you help?"

David answered quickly. "We'd be glad to come back later when we have more time and talk with you about these things!"

The woman nodded and smiled faintly. "Perhaps you will create a problem for the churches here because they will grow very big and have too many people."

At that everyone laughed. "That is the only kind of problem we ever wanted," said Alex.

The final performance came with built-in challenges. Most of the musicians couldn't extend their stay due to other engagements. But all week long we'd watched the Lord use our availability far more than our ability. So musical amateurs among us with instruments in hand were promoted to feature spots on stage and, despite the worst fears of the technical/staging director, the Lord was faithful to anoint them all. Finally, too, Jonathan was free to preach and issue an altar call. It was a glorious evening. The Lord had saved the best for last.

The next day, we received a phone call from the Office of the President of Belarus. The president had planned to attend the festival, his spokesman said, but was laid up, recovering from a back injury. Nonetheless, he wished to extend his "congratulations" on the "success of the festival," and thank Jonathan for the unity he felt it brought to the country. "For the first time in many years," said the president's spokesman, "the Jews of Belarus are holding their heads up high."

Fears about the festival inciting a Jewish civil war had apparently been allayed. The nation's non-Jews were feeling a new warmth toward the Jewish community; the Orthodox Jews did not want to jeopardize that. For the time being at least, their protests would be limited to scathing editorials in the Jewish press.

The Belarussian Minister of Culture, whose wife had stood up at the festival to commit her life to Messiah, also expressed his gratitude. (Later, through his good auspices, the State Concert Orchestra of Belarus would play at future Messianic Jewish Festivals in other CIS republics.) Additional thank you's came from the Parliament, TV networks and foreign ambassadors. Indeed, the kings' hearts had been in the hand of the Lord, directed like a watercourse as He pleased!

✧ ✧ ✧ ✧

As a result of the breaking down of dividing walls, a coupling in the Spirit had begun between Jews and Belarussians, akin to that mystery of which Ephesians speaks:

"But now in Christ Jesus you who once were far away have been brought near through the blood of Christ. For He Himself is our peace, who has made the two one and has destroyed the barrier, the dividing wall of hostility, by abolishing in His flesh the law with its commandments and regulations. His purpose was to create in Himself one new man out of the two, thus making peace, and in this one body to reconcile both of them to God through the cross, by which He put to death their hostility." (Ephesians 2:13-16)

"In reading this, then, you will be able to understand my insight into the mystery of Christ, which was not made known to men in other generations as it has now been revealed by the Spirit to God's holy apostles and prophets. *This mystery is that, through the gospel, the Gentiles are heirs together with Israel, members together of one body, and sharers together in the promise in Christ Jesus* . . . this grace was given to me: to preach to the Gentile the unsearchable riches of Christ, and to make plain to everyone the administration of this mystery, which, for ages past, was kept hidden in God, who created all things. His intent was that now, through the church, the manifold wisdom of God should be made known to the rulers and authorities in the heavenly realms, according to His eternal purpose which He accomplished in Christ Jesus our Lord. " (Ephesians 3:4-6, 8-11, emphasis added)

The profound revelation spoken of in this text is often misunderstood. It is often taken to mean that under the New Covenant, Gentiles can be saved and blessed as God's people. However, these passages refer to a *mystery*, and the fact that non-Jews could be saved was not a mystery in the Scriptures.

The Old Testament made it clear that Gentiles could serve the God of Israel and align themselves with His covenant people.[62] Isaiah 56: 6-7, for example, explains: "And foreigners who bind themselves to the Lord to serve Him...and who hold fast to My covenant, these I will bring to My holy mountain and give them joy in My house of prayer . . . for My house will be called a house of prayer for all nations." Rahab and Ruth were among those who bound themselves to the God

and people of Israel. Notice that these foreigners did not become ethnic Jews; they were fully saved and blessed *as Gentiles*.[63] Likewise,
Jesus taught that salvation in His name would extend to all nations,
as nations. He said nothing about Gentiles becoming ethnically or
"spiritually" Jewish in the process.[64] So the mystery to which Paul
refers is not about Gentiles getting saved. It is about the union of Jew
and Gentile in one newly created body of the Messiah. *It is the concept
of one new man that was never revealed in the Old Testament.*

The reconciliation of Jews and Gentiles in the body of Christ into
one new man has proved complex. The early church, of course, was
predominately Jewish. From its inception, controversy arose as to
whether Gentiles could be fully saved without submitting to Jewish
ritual. Paul set the record straight in Acts 15. Answering in the affir-
mative, he outlined only a few simple rules for Gentile converts to the
faith to follow. (Note that Paul was not implying the entire Old Testament law should be discarded as irrelevant.) His epistle to the Gentile
church in Galatia was an even more thorough indictment against the
extremist Judaizing Hebrew Christians of his time.

Today, the tables have been turned. Gentiles comprise the overwhelming majority of the church. The far more controversial issue
now is whether Jews can be saved and integrated into the body of
Christ without submitting to *Gentile* ritual. More specifically, the question is whether Jewish believers can embrace elements of their ethnic
identity and Old Testament or Hebraic-style forms of worship. Too
often, the church has answered no.[65]

Many times the church has simply and perhaps benignly regarded
the Old Testament roots of its faith as irrelevant. In other instances,
replacement doctrine has formed the basis, either consciously or
unconsciously, of its belief that born-again Jews must necessarily
disavow all vestiges of their Jewish heritage. Most commonly, the
conviction that Jews who find their Messiah must forsake their
heritage springs from a misunderstanding of the relationship between
law and grace. The New Testament and, in particular, the Book of
Galatians, condemns Jewish observance and practice only as a means
to salvation. It does not address those Jews (such as Paul himself)
who live under the New Covenant, yet observe biblical feasts and other

customs as worship—as a means of expressing their love for God precisely *because* they are saved, *not* in order to *get* saved.

Even those Jews with little interest in tradition or Old Testament observance usually find their sense of Jewish identity heightened when they come to know Messiah. They desire to worship Yeshua in a biblically Jewish context. The church's lack of understanding can leave them feeling confused and excluded, and eventually separated again by dividing walls.

To break down these walls and worship in a manner authentic to them, Jewish believers around the world have formed Messianic congregations. A good number of these Messianic Jews have embraced many or even most of the rabbinic traditions that do not contradict Scripture. Such a lifestyle, they feel, enhances their relationship with God and fulfills their calling as Jews.[66]

For the most part, Messianic congregations have sought to embrace Gentile believers and include them in their membership. Sometimes they have connected well to the larger body of Christ, serving to help restore the Jewish roots of the Christian faith to the local church community.

The Messianic congregational movement is a relatively recent phenomenon. It has flourished since 1967, the same year, incidentally, that Jerusalem came back under Jewish rule. Interestingly, its modern-day roots trace back to the former Soviet Union.

It was in the early 1800's, in the city of Kishinev, capital of Moldova, that the "Israelites of the New Covenant" came into existence. The congregation held public worship services, mostly in Hebrew, with a highly evangelistic thrust.[67] (At the same time, the Zionist aliyah movement was gaining impetus in Europe. The matter is not one of coincidence; remember that the Jews' physical restoration in Israel is tied to their spiritual restoration in Messiah.)

The evangelical church abroad took note of what was happening. In 1888, it was said in Denmark that the movement was a "sign in church history," and its purposes "so consonant with the prophetic testimony of the Bible . . . that [it] ought to be able to count upon the love and prayers of all who share with [it] something of Paul's love for the nation of Israel."[68] Attestations of support came from Christians in Europe and America—as well as opposition from the synagogues and Orthodox churches in Moldova. But words weren't enough to sustain the fledgling group. A major pogrom on Easter Day in 1903 ensured its eradication. These rabid, anti-Semitic killings targeted the whole of Kishinev's Jewish population. Believers in Yeshua were not spared.

A second Messianic congregation formed in Kishinev in the 1920's. It grew significantly in strength and impact, establishing its own local school, magazine, and even official cemetery plots. In 1930, it formally affiliated with the International Hebrew Christian Alliance, predecessor to the present-day Messianic Jewish Alliance. But this congregation met with a fate similar to that of the first. The "Church of Christian Jews of the New Covenant" was liquidated by the Nazis during World War II.[69]

Jesus said the gates of hell would not prevail against His church. Once more, in 1993, a Messianic congregation formed in Kishinev. (Just three years later, it would host a Messianic Jewish Festival, having already laid a foundation that would result in a great harvest for the whole city.)

While Messianic congregations have mushroomed around the world in recent years, countless numbers of Jewish believers do not affiliate with them. Instead, they have happily assimilated into Gentile churches. The Hebraic traditions, rituals and observances, they say, are distracting to their focus on Christ. Other Jewish Christians could be placed at various points between the two extremes, observing, for example, the biblical feasts but not keeping kosher. As would be expected, each "camp" has its own theological perspective.

Jewish believers in Messianic congregations typically feel called to present a corporate witness to their unsaved brethren. The majority of Jews still regard the claims of Christ as inherently inapplicable to them for no reason other than they were born Jewish. Thus, Messianic congregations seek to demonstrate that a Jew can believe in Jesus and still be a Jew. As Paul said in I Corinthians 9:20, "To the Jews I became like a Jew to win the Jews. To those under the law, I became like one under the law (though I myself am not under the law), so as to win those under the law." Messianic Jews justify their focus on Jewish evangelism on the grounds that most of the rest of the church has little or no dedication to it at all. If they don't labor on behalf of the salvation of their own people, nobody will.

The Bible teaches that Gentiles have been called to provoke the Jews to jealousy. (Romans 11:11) Many Christians have, in fact, taken this call seriously. They have laid their lives down for the Jewish people. We owe them a huge debt of gratitude. On the other hand, some non-Jews with a heart for Israel are so concerned about not offending the Jewish people that they never truthfully share the gospel with them at all.[70] This is somewhat puzzling. One cannot help but ask whether, if these good folks genuinely loved the Jews, they would not care more about their eternal destiny than their temporal good will.

Usually such folks are sensitive enough to know that often Jews in the West associate Christianity with anti-Semitism. So they set out to communicate respect and unconditional acceptance by building bridges of understanding. They assure the Jews their intent is not to convert them but to love them. Again, however, this is somewhat oxymoronic, unless what is meant is that the Holy Spirit is the converter of souls. Hopefully these brothers and sisters at least intercede aggressively for the salvation of their Jewish friends.[71]

How many other Christians view the Jew primarily as a prophetic timepiece rather than a human being created and loved by God—but doomed to destruction apart from Messiah? And what of those believers who insist God has an alternate plan of salvation for the Jews? Do they wishfully think Jesus didn't really mean it when he told a Jewish audience that none of them could come to the Father but through Him? (John 14:6)

The issues get even thornier. Among Gentile believers, often the distinction is blurred between the people of Israel, that is the physical descendants of Abraham, Isaac and Jacob, and the geographical land of Israel. Christians eager to support "Israel" can unwittingly turn all their attention to the Jewish State and, in so doing, actually undermine their own efforts to bless the Jewish people. They fail to realize that any ministry which supports or even openly sympathizes with Messianic Judaism will be unable to maintain a friendly relationship with the Israeli or traditional Jewish community. The well-meaning ministry must choose to support either their brothers and sisters in the faith, or the unsaved. Sadly, usually the choice is made to maintain a relationship with the unsaved Israeli or Jewish community.[72] In the meantime, if a Jew should, despite everything, manage to come to faith through this ministry, the same organization must cut him off at that point. This can leave the new believer, who likely already faces persecution for his faith by his family, friends and co-workers, fending for himself and bewildered.

A Jew in Israel can lose all he has, including even his citizenship, for believing in Jesus.[73] Most Israeli Messianic congregations endure persecution regularly. They are much in need of strengthening. They have historically received little help from the rest of the body of Christ, either in the land or abroad. The support of well-meaning Christian ministries typically is going instead to a system and/or government that persecutes its indigenous church. These Christian ministries are, in effect, not only turning their backs on the victimized Jewish church. They are supporting and encouraging their persecutors.

The Bible, however, admonishes believers to love and support fellow members of the household of faith.[74] Our loyalty must be first to the Lord, and then to other believers—especially those persecuted for their faith.

The Bible also exhorts Gentile believers to remember their Israeli Jewish brethren who are lacking materially: "For Macedonia and Achaia were pleased to make a contribution for the poor among the saints in Jerusalem. They were pleased to do it and, indeed, they owe it to them. For if the Gentiles have shared in the Jews' spiritual blessings, they owe it to the Jews to share with them their material blessings." (Romans 15:26-27)

Furthermore, it is generally recognized that the most effective evangelism of a people group results when indigenous believers are empowered to reach their own. Why should we not expect this to be the case with the Jewish people? Although God will yet sovereignly deal with unsaved Israel, possibly the most effective way that the Gentile church can support and love that nation according to the biblical mandate is to help empower their indigenous Messianic communities, both in the Diaspora and the land.

These issues rose to the fore in Minsk when the Israeli Embassy tried to cancel the festival. God had given a love for the Jewish people to the church that sponsored our activities. But indirectly they incurred the ire of the Jewish community by supporting a Messianic event. They were then faced with a choice. They could support either the representatives of mainstream rabbinic Judaism, or us. They courageously chose to support their brothers and sisters in the faith, empowering us in what manner they could to reach our people—as well as their countrymen. (Incidentally, God blessed them with special favor from the Religious Affairs Committee after the festival.)

Divisions are rarely caused by one party alone. In our attempt to attain to unity of Jew and Gentile, Jewish believers have made some mistakes as well. Some Messianic congregations have followed in the footsteps of predecessor churches in excluding those different from them. Many Gentiles with a God-given love for Israel say they have been made to feel like second-class citizens in some Messianic fellowships. Worship that began as biblically Hebraic, some say, has turned into legalistic formalism.

At the same time, Jewish believers who feel led to stay in a church often face contention from Messianic brethren insisting they could not possibly be in God's will. Despite our efforts, dividing walls have sometimes been solidified in pride, rather than torn down in humility. Have we committed the same sin as our rabbinic brethren, neglecting Israel's fundamental call to embrace and serve the nations (Gentiles), in love and humility, to the glory of God?[75]

We would do well to bear in mind God's ultimate purpose in creating in Christ one new man. Ephesians 3 states His intent is to reveal and display, in all of creation, His glory and grace through a redeemed body of Jew and Gentile. As this age draws to a close, *that* is the divine destiny for which the Spirit of God is grooming the church and Israel, side by side.

5

Kiev: Life from the Dead

"The hand of the Lord was upon me, and He brought me out by the spirit of the Lord and set me in the middle of a valley; it was full of bones. Then He said to me: 'Son of man, these bones are the whole house of Israel. They say, 'Our bones are dried up, our hope is gone; we are cut off.' Therefore prophesy and say to them, 'This is what the Sovereign Lord says: O My people, I am going to open your graves and bring you up from them; I will bring you back to the land of Israel. Then you, My people, will know that I am the Lord, when I open your graves and bring you up from them. I will put My spirit in you and you will live...'" Ezekiel 37:1, 11-14

IN THE FALL OF 1941, my maternal great grandparents, their children and their children's children were living in Kiev, Ukraine. The German army had just stormed and occupied the city. On September 28, notices were posted ordering all Jews in the region to report the next day, allegedly for purposes of resettlement. The Jews were to bring all their valuables, clothing and food sufficient for three days' journey. Rumor (planted by the Nazis) had it that the Jews would be deported to Palestine. According to the posts, failure to comply with the order would be punished by death.[76]

On the appointed day, my family was among the thousands who assembled across from the city's Jewish cemetery, at a field known as *Babi Yar* ("Grandmother's Ravine"). There the Jews were divided into groups of about one hundred and told to completely undress. Next, the Nazis collected all their parcels. Ukrainian troops assisted in nearly every phase of the operation.[77]

According to official Nazi documents and eyewitness accounts, the Jews were forced to line up, naked, one group at a time, along the rim of a large ravine. Without warning, machine guns opened fire on them. Continuously for two days, from sunrise to sunset, the Nazis systematically shot a group at a time, buried the bodies in the ravine with a thin layer of dirt and went on to the next group. Thousands of children were thrown in the pit alive, as gunfire aimed hurriedly at the victims' heads missed the little ones. [78] So many were buried alive, witnesses said, that the ground around the ravine moved for two days after the shooting stopped.

Presumably to break the monotony, some of the victims were forced to run back and forth around the ravine until they dropped from exhaustion. At that point, hungry guard dogs were unleashed on them. Others were beaten with shovels, clubs and sticks in a sadistic frenzy. Drunken soldiers laughed with amusement. Meanwhile, like a macabre film score, lively music played in the background, purportedly to muffle the unrelenting screams.[79]

The Babi Yar massacre of September 29-30, 1941, claimed the lives of 33,771 Jews, far surpassing the number killed per day at the Auschwitz and Treblinski death camps. With the willing, often glad help of contingent Ukrainian troops, the gruesome executions went on at the abyss for a year. During that time, another 65,000 civilians, most of whom were Jewish, were brutally murdered.[80]

Finally, when their defeat appeared imminent, the German army ordered Ukrainian prisoners to excavate and exhume all human remains at Babi Yar. It took several weeks to incinerate the corpses. Any bones still remaining were crushed, mixed with earth and scattered over the area. Virtually all traces of mass burial were thereby neatly erased.[81]

The Jews of Kiev, as well as those in the rest of the Soviet Union, were uninformed and ill prepared when the Germans invaded. Having signed a non-aggression pact with Hitler, Stalin ordered the Soviet press not to publish reports of anti-Semitic Nazi atrocities. As a result, Soviet Jews were generally unaware of the fate that awaited them. Consequently they made no special effort to escape.[82]

It is not widely known that approximately one third of the six million Jews killed in the Holocaust were living under Soviet rule at the onset of World War II.[83] Even after the war, the USSR was loathe to admit to the horrors inflicted upon its Jewish citizens, particularly at Babi Yar.[84]

My grandmother, Bubby, emigrated to America many years before Babi Yar. She had hoped to work hard and save enough money to enable at least some other family members across the sea to join her. She married young, however, and soon had four children of her own to care for. My grandfather worked day and night to make ends meet. Then the Depression hit. The extra money was never to be had. Instead, one day shortly after the United States entered the war, Bubby received a letter from a former neighbor in Kiev. In it she was told of the tragedy that had befallen her family at Babi Yar. Bubby died when I was still a child. She never talked to me about the incident. I suppose she felt it was one of those things which "was better you should never have to know."

Unlike my kindly grandmother, the tiny Midwestern Jewish community in which I grew up didn't pander to children's sensibilities. The synagogue made sure we knew all about the Holocaust by the time we reached kindergarten. Time and time again, we were shown reams of film footage—unedited—of concentration camp rescues, Nazi "medical' experiments, and excavations of heaps upon heaps of corpses.

The synagogue had an urgent message to Jewish baby boomers in the Midwest. "This is what the Christian world will do to you if you let them. Never again let them. *Never again!*"

"I won't," I vowed under my breath.

There weren't many Jews in our neighborhood. The few of us who lived there endured a fair amount of overt anti-Semitism. My own grade school years were replete with verbal and physical harassment for being, as the kids my age put it, a "dirty Jew." True to my vow, however, I learned how to fight—and pretty well—until puberty, when the boys suddenly got bigger and stronger.

Since "Christ-killer pig" was among the more regularly hurled accusations during these altercations, I naturally assumed Christ didn't like me one bit. Certainly those who said they belonged to Him didn't. Like they said in synagogue, it seemed the "Christians" I knew were my enemies and wanted me dead. So Christ, I assumed, was my enemy, too.

In college I encountered a new form of anti-Semitism. Christians called it "evangelism." It was the 1970's and, like many of my generation, I was searching for truth. Some of the kids on campus insisted Jesus was the Truth. Determined to silence their claims, I purchased a worn-out King James Bible at a used book store, sat down with a legal pad and proceeded to draft my arguments against Christianity. I decided to start at the beginning with the Book of Matthew and read straight through to the end. I figured I could finish over a couple of weekends.

I was appalled, however, at the first chapter, then the second and the third. The New Testament was a Jewish book! Furthermore, its very words seemed strangely alive, as if charged with love and power. In my search for truth, I'd gone through several of the sacred writings of different Eastern sects, but the Bible was different from any other religious book I'd read. I forged ahead, reading from beginning to end, with no refutation. I did have many questions, answered in the months to come by a very patient Christian neighbor. A year later, she led me in a prayer by which I committed my life to Christ.

At the time I didn't know of any other Jews who believed in Jesus. Nonetheless I experienced an instantly revitalized sense of Jewish identity. At last I knew the God of Abraham, Isaac and Jacob. I could have a relationship with Him like the patriarchs and prophets! He actually loved me and enabled me to love Him back! Life took on new meaning, serving Jesus Christ.

At the same time, I experienced instant opposition to my faith from family and friends. I'd learned as a child, however, to hold my ground for being a Jew; how much more, aided by the Holy Spirit, should I stand firm in being a Christian. When I felt lonely or sorry for myself in those early months, I imagined having the company of the Apostle Paul as I read and re-read his letters. It was a little foolish but, other than the Lord Himself, I knew Paul would understand what I was going through. God had given him the strength to endure trials far worse than mine. That gave me courage and hope.

Over the years, I eventually met other Jewish believers in Jesus (one of whom I married) and, by October 1994, I was in Kiev with dozens of Messianic missionaries. It was in that city that an unshakable nudging compelled me to visit Babi Yar.

The Holocaust had long ago ceased to be a focus of my life. Yeshua had lovingly healed the bitter wounds of anti-Semitism in my soul. It had been a long process, leaving me with no desire to dig up old memories or stories. So I wasn't sure why I needed to go to Babi Yar. At least, however, I wasn't alone. Several of my teammates had sensed the same peculiar pull to this notorious place. We set out together one morning, suspecting a divine appointment awaited us there.

It was a clear, cold autumn day. The park in which the ravine was located was strangely still when we arrived. Our group, too, was uncharacteristically quiet. The only sound to be heard, apart from muffled traffic in the distance, was the rhythmic crunching of browned leaves underfoot as we walked contemplatively to the infamous site. Eventually we came upon an impressive memorial, recently erected, in the form of a menorah (Jewish ceremonial candelabrum). Nearby stood a cluster of white-barked birch trees and thick, gnarled foliage. Behind it lay the death pit.

Babi Yar looked so surprisingly ordinary, even pretty, as to be maddening. Lush bushes and trees had sprung up throughout the inside of the ravine. *The ground cover works well*, I thought, angered at evil's deceptive veneer.

Our group agreed to separate for a short time to meditate individually before the Lord. I found a secluded spot next to the end of the pit and sat down on a gnarled tree trunk. For the next hour or so, the past and present blurred eerily into timelessness. *So this is the place I've heard so much about, the place saturated by the blood and flesh of my own flesh and blood.* I picked up a handful of the dry black dirt lining the rim. It was speckled with countless tiny white flecks. *Powdered bones? Ashes of burnt corpses? My relatives? The remains of my people, my God's people?*

Death's haunt emanated from the ravine, however history might try to hide beneath the attractive greenery. A shroud of doom hung in the air. The blood and bones of humanity still screamed to heaven, hell and earth. Only the blood of Messiah could ever silence it.

Feeling so close to death, it seemed a small miracle that I should exist at all. Had Bubby not been the one her family chose to send to America, I would never be. A twinge of survivor guilt crept over me.

Then I remembered the old childhood admonition. "This is what the Christian world will do to *you . . .*"

I knew the Holocaust defied rational human explanation. It had been supernaturally masterminded and effected by the devil himself. Satan's timeless hatred of the Jews flows from his hatred of God. Because he opposes the Sovereign One, he opposes God's covenant people. He also hates and opposes God's plan for the redemption of humanity and, in that plan, the Jews play an integral role.

The devil's first line of opposition since the fall of Adam and Eve has been deception. Deceived men become tools in his hands. They are capable of destroying themselves, a whole nation, even the world. The combined lies of anti-Semitism and Aryan supremacy are but two examples of hell's heinous ploys for destruction.

As well as I thought I, a sophisticated American of the 90's, could explain the Holocaust, I needed more at that moment at Babi Yar's edge. I needed to know: *How could a truly loving and all-powerful God have let this happen?*

I waited in silence, hearing only an occasional crunch of leaves as one of my companions strolled nearby. With a sorrow of soul too heavy to formulate into words, I opened my Bible to the Book of Lamentations. The anguished cry of the prophet Jeremiah eloquently expressed what weighed on my heart:

"This is why I weep and my eyes over flow with tears . . . Without pity the Lord has swallowed up all the dwellings of Jacob; in His wrath, He has torn down the strongholds of the Daughter of Judah. He has brought her kingdom and its princes down to the ground in dishonor. The Lord has done what He planned; He has fulfilled His word, which He decreed long ago. He has overthrown you without pity, He has let the enemy gloat over you, He has exalted the horn of your foes . . ."

"Yet this I call to mind and therefore I have hope: Because of the Lord's great love we are not consumed, for His compassions never fail . . . For He does not willingly bring affliction or grief to the children of men . . . Let us examine our ways and test them, and let us return to the Lord . . . My eyes will flow unceasingly without relief, until the Lord looks down from heaven and sees . . ." (Lamentations 2-3)

I flipped back in the Scriptures to the blessings and curses set before Israel as the nation entered the Promised Land. "If you do not obey the Lord your God and do not carefully follow all His commands and decrees I [Moses] am giving you today, all these curses will come upon you and overtake you . . ." (Deuteronomy 28:15) Among "all these curses" is genocide. (Deuteronomy 28:37, 45-66)

Who among us could say we, the Jews, have "carefully followed all His commands and decrees" given us that day? Instead we have sinned grievously against our God—and reaped the prophetic consequences.

Yet the Bible teaches that when God disciplines Israel it is with justice—never malice. Jeremiah 46:28 says, "Though I completely destroy all the nations among which I scatter you, I will not completely destroy you. I will discipline you but only with justice; I will not let you go entirely unpunished." *Thus, however abominable Israel's sin, it offers no excuse for the nations' malevolent persecution of her people.*

The Scriptures speak of divine judgment to fall upon those who would justify their mistreatment of Israel based on her sin. Ezekiel 35:15 says: "Because you rejoiced when the inheritance of the house of Israel became desolate, that is how I will treat you." Jeremiah prophesies the Lord's vengeance on Babylon for the same reason: "Whoever found them [scattered Israel] devoured them; their enemies said, 'We are not guilty, for they sinned against the Lord, their true pasture, the Lord, the hope of their fathers.' . . . Because you rejoice and are glad, you who pillage My inheritance . . . she who gave you birth will be disgraced...Since this is the vengeance of the Lord, take vengeance on her; do to her as she has done to others . . . All who pass [you] will be horrified and scoff because of all your wounds." (Jeremiah 50: 7, 11-13)

Even the nations that do not actively seek Israel's harm but passively do nothing to prevent it are guilty in God's eyes. "On the day you stood aloof while strangers carried off [Israel's] wealth and foreigners entered his gates and cast lots for Jerusalem, you were like one of them." (Obadiah 1:11)

I gazed down again at the death pit, feeling even more fully the weight of its indictment against humanity. My thoughts ventured to the outer limits of man's depravity. At the same time, I remembered that the rebirth of the nation of Israel came just seven years after Babi Yar, out of the ashes of the Holocaust. God had a purpose in the suffering. However heinous the tribulation in the world, Messiah Jesus had overcome it . . .

How magnificently the power of the cross of Yeshua radiated that moment at Babi Yar! What depth of divine love that canceled the curse condemning fallen man: "Surely He took up our infirmities and carried our sorrows, yet we considered Him stricken by God, smitten by Him and afflicted. But He was pierced for our transgressions, He was crushed for our iniquities; the punishment that brought us peace was upon Him, and by His wounds we are healed. We all, like sheep, have gone astray, each of us has turned to his own way; and the Lord has laid on Him the iniquity of us all." (Isaiah 53: 4-6)

I picked up another handful of earth. *May the power of the blood of Messiah cleanse and heal this place*, I petitioned. *Oh Lord, bring justice to the earth!* [85]

It was getting late. The sound of crunching leaves and somber voices interrupted my thoughts as my friends gathered nearby. It was time to join them.

My teammates, too, had been stirred to the core. Avner, the festival's street outreach director, had responded dramatically. He had felt led of the Lord to walk down, then climb out of, the pit in a prophetic re-enactment of Ezekiel 37:1-14. In that passage, Ezekiel sees a valley of dry bones. The Lord breathes on them, attaches flesh to them and brings them to life. Then he says to Ezekiel:

"Son of man, these bones are the whole house of Israel. They say, 'Our bones are dried up and our hope is gone. We are cut off.' Therefore prophesy and say to them: 'This is what the Sovereign Lord says: "O My people, I am going to open your graves and bring you up from them; I will bring you back to the land of Israel. Then you, My people, will know that I am the Lord, when I open your graves and bring you up from them.

I will put My Spirit in you and you will live, and I will settle you in your own land. Then you will know that I, the Lord, have spoken and I have done it," declares the Lord.'" (Ezekiel 37:11-14)

Moved by Avner's response, the rest of us went before the Lord as one, praying for the fulfillment of Ezekiel's vision. Together we cried out in repentance and intercession, in mourning and hope. We believed God for an outpouring of mercy, for the blood of the Lamb to cover the bloodshed of man.

As we prayed, the Light of Life streamed upon that chilling pit of death. Suddenly, in its radiance, disjointed shadows of my own past were focused and blended into divine redemption. It was the cross of Yeshua that declared "Never again!" It was the cross that set "free those who all their lives were held in slavery by their fear of death." (Hebrews 2:15)

My friends and I left Babi Yar expecting the Lord to "open up the graves" of Kiev that week. We believed God would resurrect Israel's dry bones, reviving the Jewish people of that city. In some way this would mean life from the dead for their Ukrainian countrymen as well. Later that day, an encounter with two Holocaust survivors, a Jewish man named Soltan and a Gentile woman named Anna, proved foretelling.

✧   ✧   ✧   ✧

Soltan, an aging widower, lived far from Kiev. He was on his way to Israel, he explained, but needed to spend a few days in the city to obtain his exit visa and papers for aliyah.

Soltan's heart had already been sovereignly softened by the Spirit of God. When our workers shared the gospel with him, he wanted to give his life to Yeshua immediately. "I felt fire all through my body when we prayed and very great happiness," Soltan told them excitedly.

Soltan had survived four years in the concentration camps of Auschwitz and Nordhausen, where his last job was to carry corpses away from the death ovens. He said he could not forget the screaming he heard in those places. He still hears it in his head, he said, especially at night when it is very quiet.

The team members who led Soltan to the Lord treated him to a stay at our hotel for a few days while he waited for his documents to be processed. There he met a festival worker from Germany, a non-Jew who took him under her wing for the duration of the week. Soltan spoke Yiddish, a language similar to German, so the two were able to communicate well. But he could not understand why everyone, especially the German woman, was being so good to him.

"It is an honor for me as a German to help you, even a little bit," explained his new friend.

"No," Soltan replied, shaking his head. "Nobody can choose into what nationality he is born. You did not choose to be German. I did not choose to be Jewish. So it is not your fault what happened many years go."

Soltan had found the courage to forgive and be forgiven—a token of resurrected dry bones. At the same time, a handful of other outreach workers were meeting a Ukrainian woman named Anna. Anna had been designated by the State of Israel as a "Righteous Gentile."[86] She and her mother had risked their lives to rescue Jewish friends during the Nazi occupation of Kiev. But over the decades, Anna's life had grown obscure and lonely. The outreach workers who met Anna were eager to hear her story. With typical Ukrainian hospitality, she invited them to her flat for the afternoon.

During world War II, Anna's mother was close friends with a Jewish woman named Maya (not her real name). Maya was an obstetrician and Anna was best friends with her daughter, Rachel. Maya had been warned to leave Kiev because the Germans were coming but she had many pregnant patients and was unwilling to abandon them.

When the orders came to round up the Jews at Babi Yar, Anna's mother hid Maya and Rachel in their house. After a year, neighbors reported them to the authorities. Anna and her mother quickly switched passport photos with Maya and Rachel, both of whom looked Ukrainian. They sent them to live with Anna's grandmother in the country, where both mother and daughter waited out the war in safety.

When the Nazis came to the house and couldn't find the Jews, they arrested Anna and her mother. The two were deported to a labor camp in Poland. A year later, they were released rather miraculously when a Nazi guard noticed they didn't look Jewish and asked why they were there. A mistake had been made with passports, they said. Once freed, Anna and her mother ran into a nearby forest and hid. Eventually they made their way home on foot.

Years after, Anna fell in love with and married a Jewish man. But she could never bring herself to take his last name for fear of anti-Semitism. Now a widow, she lived alone and was very poor, unable to afford even a telephone. Rachel was still her best friend, she said. It was Rachel who had seen to it that Anna was honored as a Righteous Gentile.

The festival workers who visited Anna shared the love of Yeshua with her. They left her a Ukrainian Bible, groceries, a bouquet of flowers and some cash. The gifts were to thank her, they said, for her sacrificial kindness so many years ago. Even more importantly, they wanted Anna to know about the One who had sacrificed His life to rescue her. Anna was already a God-fearing woman, perhaps even a nominal believer, but now, she said, she knew God had not forsaken her. She wanted to come to the festival, she added, because all of Kiev needed God's love.

✧ ✧ ✧ ✧

Kiev's need of God's love was evidenced in part by the city's resistance to it. By our trip in 1994, the government was beginning to clamp down on religious freedoms, particularly with respect to foreign nondenominational church groups. For this reason, the Ukrainian Committee of Religious Affairs had rejected our initial application to put on the festival, even after we'd obtained all the approvals they wanted from their various state-registered churches.

Festival organizers appealed to the Parliament. The Parliament referred us to the Ministry of Cultural Affairs. As in Belarus, the authorities determined the festival was cultural in nature because it was Jewish, despite its patently religious content. So, after months of bureaucratic delays, reshuffling and more delays, the Ministry of Cultural Affairs finally gave us their approval. Then, two weeks before the festival, the Religious Affairs Committee tried to revoke it.

The Religious Committee protested first to the Cultural Affairs people, then to the Parliament. When their efforts proved unsuccessful, they started threatening the concert hall director. The week of the festival we were still getting distraught calls from him, as well as the Mayor's Office and the Ministry of the Interior. Two days before opening night, the Ministry of Cultural Affairs phoned, giving notice of the festival's probable cancellation and implicating the source of the opposition.

The Orthodox Jewish community in Kiev was well organized, we learned. Aided by anti-missionaries from New York, they were determined not to allow a repeat of our experience in Minsk. This time they planned to make sure the authorities wouldn't change their minds.

Jonathan was allowed to attend a so-called hearing concerning the cancellation of the festival. He and Alex could present their case at the Mayor's office. In the meantime, the rest of us prayed hard: "Summon Your power, O God; show us Your strength, O God, as You have done before!" (Psalm 68:28)

Awaiting Jonathan and Alex downtown were representatives from the Cultural Affairs Committee, the Mayor's office, the concert hall and the Orthodox Jewish community. Also present was the director of the Ukrainian Jewish Council, Mr. Levin (not his real name). Mr. Levin was the highest ranking representative of the Jewish community in the country. In the slew of phone calls and complaints, nobody had mentioned his name, but it was clear that Mr. Levin was the one calling the shots.

"This festival is a national Jewish event," he said gruffly to Jonathan and Alex. "All national Jewish events in Ukraine must be approved by the Ukrainian Jewish Council. You never got our approval."

"Nobody ever told us about your Council," Jonathan replied, glancing at the Cultural Affairs representative. "We were told we had all the approvals we needed."

The Orthodox Jewish community's representative, Igor, sat fidgeting next to Mr. Levin, muttering something in his ear every few seconds. Levin brushed him aside with a sweep of his hand and frowned at Jonathan.

"You do not have our approval so you do not have what you need.

We do not approve of certain things you are doing."

"Perhaps you can tell us what you don't approve of," Alex offered.

Fists clenched and red in the face, Igor could no longer contain himself. Jumping up from his seat, he shouted, "We do not approve of the destruction of Jewish souls! We will not allow this event, this heresy, to take place!"

Levin's anger turned from Jonathan to Igor. Jonathan noticed there appeared to be little affection between the two. "The whole city is planning to go to this festival," he snapped back. "If we cancel it now, they will be upset and blame the Jews. Is that what you want?"

Igor sat down in silence. Jonathan and Alex stared at each other in near disbelief. Mr. Levin continued. "We will tell you what we do not approve of. If you agree to our requirements, we will give you permission for the festival.

"First of all, you must stop all advertising immediately. You have done too much. So much advertising supports the myth about Jews controlling the media."

Jonathan knew the advertising had been extensive, albeit for the sake of proclaiming the name of Yeshua. By now, several of the TV and radio stations were following the festival on their own. "We will stop all the advertising," he agreed.

"You must not hand out any more literature in public. Not on the streets and not at the festival. It is like forcing propaganda on people."

Jonathan thought quickly for a moment. The evangelism teams could easily shift their focus to street preaching and home visits, but they'd brought 15,000 copies of books and discipleship materials to distribute at the festival. The ex-Soviets loved Christian literature because it was not widely available to them. They gladly shared it with their family and friends, which made it a very effective evangelism tool. "Can we leave the literature out on tables at the festival?" he asked. "Then people could pick them up if they wanted to, and nobody would force it on them."

Levin grimaced. "Well...if nobody forces it on them . . . Yes, I suppose that would be all right."

Igor squirmed in his seat and started turning red again.

Levin continued with his list. "It is very important that at the festival you do not tell the Jews to leave Ukraine. Some groups have come here and said we should leave because there will be pogroms again. This only hurts our relationship with the Ukrainians. Instead, you must mention that some Ukrainians helped Jews during the Holocaust."

"I understand," Jonathan said, sympathizing with Levin's sensitive position.

"Also, there are hundreds of Holocaust survivors in Kiev. We want you to honor them at the festival with special seats and a reception. There should be food at this reception—good food. And we want you to donate something to them. The newspapers say you brought half a ton of medicine to distribute. You must give some medicine to our survivors."

Jonathan was practically incredulous. Levin wanted the Holocaust survivors to go to the festival—so much so that he would insist on a special reception? Plus provide the opportunity to bless them with medical aid? Whatever was going on here, he had to respond quickly, before Igor disrupted things. "It would be an honor for us to honor them . . ."

As if on cue, Igor started muttering again in Levin's ear.

"The last requirement is that, since this is a cultural event, you must not give a religious sermon."

At this, Jonathan flinched. "But Mr. Levin, in all our literature and advertisements, we have promised people we would tell them about the Messiah."

Levin frowned and leaned his face on the palm of his hand. "I watched their video of the festival in Moscow," interjected the Cultural Affairs representative. "Even though this is clearly a cultural event, the part I liked best was the sermon. It is a message our people need to hear. It can bring no harm to Ukraine."

Levin thought quietly for a moment, then looked appeased. "All right, you may tell them about the Messiah, but you must not try to convert them to Orthodoxy."

By now, Jonathan wondered if Alex was translating the conversation right. "We will definitely not try to convert them to Orthodoxy. We will only tell them about the Jewish Messiah," he replied.

Igor was indignant. "They're going to talk about Jesus being the Messiah! You *know* that!" he shouted at Levin. "If you let them do that, we will protest!" Igor's fist hit the table. "Our people will stand in front of the concert hall and save Jewish souls from this lie . . ."

The deputy mayor interrupted. "Are you threatening to disturb the peace of the city? Is this what you're planning to do?"

"Igor, they've agreed to everything else we demanded. We have to be willing," said Levin, "to give in a little on something."

Igor sank sullenly in his seat while everyone else in the room exchanged nodding glances. "All right, then, we have an agreement," Levin flatly announced. Turning to Jonathan he added, "The Ukrainian Jewish Council gives permission, and is now the official sponsor of, this Messianic Jewish Festival. I will inform the rabbis."

And so it was, as far as we know, that the Jewish community of Ukraine became the first in the world to officially sponsor an event declaring the Messiahship of Yeshua.

Igor slipped out of the room while the papers were drawn up. According to the documents, the Ukrainian Jewish Council's consent was conditioned on our adherence to the terms of the negotiated agreement. Failure to comply would result in the festival's cancellation. Marveling at the Lord's goodness and might, Jonathan shook Mr. Levin's hand and thanked him for his support.

Levin answered matter-of-factly. We do not have to let the Orthodox Jews run things here. Most of the Jews in this country do not agree with them. I, for one, have read your literature and feel closer to you than to them." Hesitatingly he added, "But it is important to keep peace."

Jonathan and Alex returned from the battle elated. God had triumphed and the whole team celebrated the victory. Finally, things were under control . . . or so it seemed . . .

The first day of the festival was filled with the usual flurry of last minute details and late-breaking technical problems. In the midst of the hubbub, only a few hours before the concert was scheduled to begin, another call came from city officials. This time, we were told that, due to our breach of yesterday's agreement with the Ukrainian Jewish Council, the festival was canceled. One of our ads had allegedly aired that morning over the public address system of the city's Metro.

Together with an entourage of team leaders, Jonathan and Alex dashed off to the Mayor's office. Early that morning, they had carefully instructed the Metro administration in no uncertain terms to stop all the ads. Had one slipped out by mistake?

On the way downtown, Jonathan mentally rehearsed his case: If an ad had aired, it was beyond our control. Over 200 foreigners on the team had come to Kiev—with medical aid. The festival was our free gift to the city. We had done no one any harm. Thousands of people were expecting the concert to begin in only a few hours. Was this the way a democratic government treated people?

TV cameras and newsmen were waiting outside city hall. Inside, general confusion reigned. As best as could be discerned, the Orthodox Jews had complained about the airing of a Metro ad, but the complaint could not be verified. As a result, conflicting instructions had been given to the concert hall director and city militia about canceling the festival. Nobody was quite sure who had given what orders to whom or for what reason. Mr. Levin and Igor were there, arguing with each other and trying to unravel the story. In the midst of the chaos, Jonathan couldn't get a word in.

The bickering dragged on for some time before the officials decided they'd had enough. Finally, an exasperated-looking deputy mayor interrupted and flatly declared, "There has obviously been a mistake. The festival is not going to be canceled." And as if the whole thing had been nothing more than a puff of smoke, it evaporated into the air. "The enemies of the Lord will vanish—like smoke they vanish away . . ." (Psalms 37:20, NAS)

✧　✧　✧　✧

When the air cleared, we turned our attention to our specially honored festival guests, the Holocaust survivors. How privileged we were to host the pre-concert buffet for them! Only the Lord could have masterminded this opportunity.

Avner warmly welcomed the group of about 100 in Yiddish, a language they understood well. He explained that his own family, some of whom had perished in the Holocaust, had come from Kiev. The survivors listened intently. He invited them to enjoy the food set out on the tables as well as the spiritual banquet at the concert. "Our hope is that, in some way, the sorrow and pain of the Holocaust will be replaced with the joy of the Lord tonight," he said.

Avner had barely finished his welcome when I felt a tug on my sleeve and tap on my forearm. I looked down at a woman about half my height and twice my age. This determined survivor spoke English and she had an urgent request. "Please, do you have any medicine with you? Many of us are very sick. We especially need medicines for cancer."

I felt chagrined and ashamed at that moment for not having any cancer medicine with me, as if this was something I normally carried around. "No, I'm really sorry," I replied sheepishly, "but I do have a God who is able to heal the sick. If you like, I would be glad to pray for those in your group who are ill."

To my astonishment, this alternative more than satisfied her. Her face lit up. "Yes, yes, please!"

So we prayed, and when we finished, this little lady with huge faith rejoiced, absolutely confident that now God Himself would do something. She joined her friends eating at the table, chattering at them with delight.

How tender-spirited these precious ones seemed! But how would they respond in a few short hours to the gospel of Jesus Christ? Hadn't they been led to believe it was in His name the atrocities of the Holocaust had been committed?

In our Western world, the memory of the Holocaust often stands as a garrison in the Jewish soul against the claims of Yeshua. Certainly it once did for me. Yet among these who had actually survived the horror I sensed something different. I saw hearts that had been crushed, yet remained tender, almost childlike. I sensed spiritual hunger . . .

The buffet was drawing to a close when an ear-piercing crash suddenly resounded from the downstairs lobby. A throng of several thousand had descended on the concert hall, uncomfortably reminiscent of Minsk. Tonight, however, in their zeal, the crowds had actually pushed right through and broken down one of the glass doors. Moments later, as a harried custodian boarded up the shattered door, I thought of the determined folks who once broke through the roof of a house to get a disabled friend to see Jesus. (Mark 2:4) What would that kind of spiritual desperation produce tonight?

The doors opened and the eager masses stampeded into the building. The festival organizers not involved in staging were busy either with seating the Holocaust survivors, crowd control, the broken door, or a small fire that had erupted from a smoldering cigarette in the ladies' room. *Stay calm. This is just normal life in the former Soviet Union,* I reminded myself. *The Lord is in control!*

I'd scarcely formed the words in my mind when I discovered that a bewildering bazaar had been set up in the lobby next to our literature tables. Amidst the Messiah tracts, miscellaneous Jewish artifacts were now being offered for sale. Among the goods being politely hawked were Shabbat candlesticks, *challah* (twisted bread) covers, and knit skull caps. Also advertised were the services of an experienced matchmaker, "To help you find your *beshairt* (Yiddish for "destined") one." Presumably, this makeshift mall had some connection with our sponsor, the Ukrainian Jewish Council.

Past these outer courts and inside the concert theater, however, things were surprisingly peaceful. Four thousand guests sat quietly, perusing programs and gobbling up gospel tracts. As in Moscow and Minsk, I watched expectancy on faces turn quickly to captivated curiosity with the opening song. The long-suffering people of the CIS have a remarkably childlike openness of spirit or, perhaps, it is more that they have not developed that specific hardness to the gospel characteristic of so-called post-Christian era Westerners. Whatever the case, I never tired of watching the ex-Soviets soak up the love of Jesus, like dry sponges dipped in fresh water.

The stage set sparkled with color in contrast to the gray surroundings of Kiev. Rhythmically flashing laser lights and Hebraic-costumed dancers enlivened the air of joy flowing from vibrant medleys of praise. "It looked like God gave us a party and, right on stage, opened up a brightly wrapped gift," said one of the Ukrainian Jews.

The people reacted as if they had indeed been handed a present from God. Transfixed stares gave way to slightly puzzled expressions. It seemed the good folks were searching for a mental grid on which to peg the moment. They had done nothing to earn this gift called grace, and they knew it. Unmerited favor is hard for man to comprehend, regardless of his culture or background.

The children were the first to respond. Squealing with delight, little girls in party dresses and large chiffon hair bows, together with small boys decked in tuxedos or suit jackets, ran pell mell to the front of the stage to join the dancers. Their parents followed, pulled along at the hand by older children who didn't want to be left out. Team members jumped in to lend flow and order to the hundreds of little ones dancing up and down the aisles.

Interspersed with the praise and worship songs were some of the traditional Hebrew prayers Jews have chanted for centuries around the world. Among them was the *Shema* (Hebrew for "Hear"), considered the cornerstone prayer of Judaism. It is taken from Deuteronomy 6:4: "Hear O Israel, the Lord our God, the Lord is one." Observant Jews recite the Shema three times a day. Many utter this prayer with their last breath as they enter eternity. *How many of Babi Yar's victims*, I wondered, *had perished with the Shema on their lips? Were my great-grandparents among them?*

Marty Goetz, the American musician on stage, proclaimed again the Shema's opening words, *"Shema Yisrael . . ."* ("Hear O Israel"). My mind flashed back to my visit to Babi Yar and the prophet Ezekiel's words: "Then He said to me, 'Prophesy to these bones and say to them, Dry bones, hear the word of the Lord . . . I will make breath enter you, and you will come to life.' " (Ezekiel 37:4-5)

"Adonai Eloheinu, Adonai echad . . ." ("The Lord our God, the Lord is one.") Marty went on, as if echoing the prophecy. And I could almost hear and see a rattling of the disintegrated bones at Babi Yar: "So I prophesied as I was commanded and, as I was prophesying, there was a noise, a rattling sound, and the bones came together, bone to bone . . . but there was no breath in them." (Ezekiel 37:7-8)

Marty replayed the melody on the piano with soul-penetrating intercessory power. At once, in my mind's eye, Babi Yar's dry bones came to life by the wind of the Spirit, as Ezekiel described: "Then He said to me, 'Prophesy to the breath; prophesy, son of man, and say to it, "This is what the Sovereign Lord says: Come from the four

winds, O breath, and breathe into these slain, that they may live."'
So I prophesied as He commanded me, and breath entered them; they
came to life and stood up on their feet—a vast army." (Ezekiel 37:9-10)

As the music continued, I could "see" the Jewish people of Kiev
and throughout Ukraine being spiritually resurrected from the dead—
and revived. The proclamation of the Shema had trumpeted a call to
life from the dead. "Then you, my people, will know that I am the
Lord, when I open your graves and bring you up from them. I will put
My Spirit in you and you will live . . ." (Ezekiel 37:13-14)

Before my eyes, the manifest presence of the Lord Jesus in the
concert hall, as the Resurrection and the Life, was unlike anything I'd
ever experienced. As He had once declared to a dead-and-buried friend,
Lazarus, Yeshua's commanding call to "come forth" overlaid each note
sung from the platform. A thick, tangible hush fell upon the people,
their spirits resonating with the King's cry.

A palpable sense of divine love saturated the room as closing medleys spoke of God's tender kindness and compassion. The last chorus
consisted of but one word, the same in English, Russian and Hebrew:
"Hallelujah." As this refrain was sung over and again, all rose spon-
taneously and silently to their feet. There had been no prompting of
any kind. Yet the people stood at their seats as if at attention. Some
eyes were closed, some tears were flowing, some heads were nodding.
They knew their King and Captain had come. He had breathed upon
them and, like dry bones, they had come to life and stood up on their
feet—"a vast army." It was life from the dead.

We had an altar call later that night, though clearly the Lord had
already issued His own. I was watching from the balcony when Jonathan
asked if anyone wanted to pray a prayer of repentance. I fixed my focus
on the Holocaust survivors sitting down in their reserved bloc of seats.
Nearly all stood to their feet to ask Messiah into their hearts.

As He had done long ago in a synagogue in Nazareth, that night
in a concert hall in Kiev, the Anointed One came to preach good news
to the poor, bind up the brokenhearted, and proclaim freedom to the
captives. Comforting the mourners in Zion— especially the Holocaust
survivors—He bestowed on them crowns of beauty instead of ashes,
the oil of gladness instead of mourning, and garments of praise

instead of a spirit of despair. (Luke 4:16-21; Isaiah 61:1-3)

As many as 15,000 people, half of whom were Jewish, asked Jesus into their hearts during the Kiev festival that week. An indigenous Ukrainian Jewish believer accepted the Lord's call to pastor those among them desiring to form a Messianic congregation. Over the years, the congregation has flourished, the Lord still adding to their number those being saved, and using them to impact communities throughout Ukraine with a Messianic vision.

6

Russia Revisited:
Song of the Barren

"Sing, O barren, you who have not borne. Break forth into singing, and cry aloud, you who have not travailed with child; for more are the children of the desolate than the children of the married woman,' says the Lord. 'Enlarge the place of your tent and let them stretch out the curtains of your habitations; do not spare, lengthen your cords, and strengthen your stakes. For you shall expand to the right and to the left . . .' " Isaiah 54: 1-3, NKJ

IN BIBLICAL ISRAEL, spring was the season of war. As the sun greeted and warmed the earth, battles raged. Buds and blossoms emerged, flocks multiplied and kings' armies went into combat. So it was for us.

In Russia, the spring of 1995 was unusually warm and bright. Soft purple lilacs and creamy lilies-of-the-valley blossomed all over Moscow. The skies were uncharacteristically blue. A full year had passed since the inception of Messianic Congregation Shomer Israel. We had returned to Russia to work with our new brothers and sisters on another outreach. Little did we anticipate, however, the nature of the battle awaiting us there.

Our plan was to mobilize the fledgling flock formed from last year's festival to do the work of the ministry. The goal was to bless and strengthen these zealous young believers. Another festival, it was felt, would provide opportunity for them to grow in maturity, as well as size. After the outreach in Moscow, we planned to travel to St. Petersburg, where we would organize a similar undertaking with the two-year-old fellowship in that city.

I was eager to visit the Messianic congregation in Moscow, having witnessed a bit of its birth. The day after we arrived was a Saturday, so I decided, together with some of the festival organizers, to attend their Shabbat service. We hailed a cab, piled into the back seat and, since we'd gotten off to a late start, hoped the driver wouldn't prove a stickler for the speed limit.

As usual, however, the cab driver had trouble with our directions. We were riding way too long, it seemed, and I was growing impatient. By now we would be quite late. *Look at the bright side*, I told myself as another lilac bush blurred by in the window. *Nothing happens on time in Russia, so you probably won't miss the whole service. Remember that old Russian (or was it Soviet?) proverb: (S)he who is the most patient wins.*

Eventually the cab stopped in front of a shabby theater across from a park. When we opened the door to the building, we heard muffled singing and breathed a sigh of relief. We ran up the dark flight of creaky stairs that greeted us at the entrance. The singing grew not only louder but recognizable. The congregation was fervently sounding, in Russian, the Israeli national anthem, *"HaTikvah"* (Hebrew for "The Hope"). As we opened the door a crack and tried to slip in unobtrusively, we couldn't help but feel weepy. At that moment, HaTikvah aptly symbolized the prophetic fulfillment of the Hope of Israel having reached the Land of the North. The voices of these Jewish followers of Messiah left no doubt about it.

We found empty seats among the worshippers, and I scanned the room while, next, tithes were collected. Though the auditorium which the group rented for its Shabbat service was quite austere, they had added their distinct touches. A velvet banner with "Yeshua" written in large Hebrew letters was draped across a wooden podium. A star of David and lions symbolizing the tribe of Judah bordered the "Yeshua." An Israeli flag stood at the side of the platform. It was probably one of only a few in all of the former Soviet Union.

Jeff, the evangelist turned missionary from Maryland, served as the congregation's Messianic rabbi. He preached a few words from Romans 10 about God's heart for Israel's salvation, then gave an altar call. His words were stirring. An even greater anointing seemed to come, however, through the translator, an impassioned young woman with an obvious call to preach. Three visitors went forward to repent and receive the gift of eternal life. The congregation cheered.

Jeff continued with his message, based on Matthew 4:18-22, in which the disciples forsake all to follow Christ and become fishers of men. "Are you willing to do the same?" he asked the people.

"Dah!" (Russian for "Yes!") many shouted, heads nodding and arms shooting up in the air.

"Then let's do it!" Jeff declared and the translator echoed. "For those of you who want to go fishing for souls, we're moving the service out into the street."

With that announcement, the indoor service was duly dismissed. About half the congregants followed Jeff to a city square bustling with Saturday shoppers. There they proceeded to share one-on-one with their countrymen about the love of God, using the familiar-looking festival invitations as bait. I was both proud of, and convicted by, their enthusiasm.

Out on the square I got to know one of the congregation's dedicated young couples, Sasha and his wife Sveta. Sveta, who is not Jewish, had already considered herself a born again Christian from her exposure to Russian Orthodoxy. But, as she put it, she had never been discipled. Sasha, who is Jewish, told me he came to faith right after Shomer Israel's inaugural service last year

"My parents changed my last name when I was a teenager so I could hide that I was Jewish," Sasha explained. "Because of anti-Semitism, I was trying not to think of myself as Jewish until the festival last year. Then, when I went to the first meeting of the congregation, I felt very much like I was home. From that day on, I knew I was a Jew and it (my Jewishness) became so real to me because of Yeshua."

Sasha is a dark-haired, wiry young man, an economist by profession. He wears a large star of David around his neck, as well as a *yarmulke* (skull cap). "I think when we emigrate to Israel, we will again use my real name," he said.

Sveta is a sparkling, blue-eyed blonde, lovely and graceful, even in her third trimester of pregnancy. "When I think of us a year ago, it is like it is not us. Now when we have a problem, we pray and ask God what to do. He shows us what must be changed. Our four-year-old daughter also has strong faith. Many times she tells us something that she says God has told her to say. It is very powerful and very amazing. It makes us to be humble."

Sasha and Sveta were serving steadfastly in the congregation's worship ministry. They helped lead worship at the outreach prayer meetings throughout the week. Their impassioned Russian/Hebrew praise and worship proved a welcome contrast to our imported-from-America version of the previous year.

Sasha introduced me to Sergei, who also worked with the worship team. It didn't take long to see the anointing on Sergei's life. Once out on the street, he would stop to chat with me for only few seconds at a time. A far more urgent task than fellowship was saving souls. Like Sasha, he had grown up hiding the fact he was Jewish. Sergei's official papers actually identified him as Russian (i.e., not Jewish).

Sergei had come to the festival the previous year and given his life to the Lord at Shomer Israel's first meeting. At the end of the service, one of the team leaders laid hands on him and prayed for him. Minutes later, while on his way home, Sergei came upon a crowd of people gathered around a man lying on the sidewalk. The man was having a seizure and appeared to be unconscious. Without thinking twice about it, Sergei laid hands on him and prayed the same way he'd just seen people do at the meeting. The seizure stopped, the man woke up, and it appeared he was instantly healed. "It was the first time in my life that I saw the power of God like that," he said. "It would take too long to tell you about everything, but my life got very changed."

Sergei was in the Russian Army's "spy ministry," as he put it, when he came to the festival. If this "spy ministry" ever found out he was Jewish, he said, he would be shot. He ended up leaving his lucrative career to serve in God's army instead.

These young firebrands from the CIS comprise a zealous army the likes of which are hard to find among our generation of North American believers. So it was to our delight that Scott and I were assigned evangelism teams in Moscow and St. Petersburg consisting entirely of Russians, Ukrainians and Belarussians. Most of these foot soldiers were students at the Messianic Bible school in St. Petersburg. Their childlike faith, humble boldness and purity of passion for Christ inspired and challenged us time and again.

Our assistant team leader was Eduard, a dedicated student at the Bible school and former colonel in the Soviet Army. With his distinguished shock of white hair, Eduard had an air of princely meekness about him. Ever the servant, he was always the first to volunteer for even the most mundane of tasks. When one of the women on our team was physically accosted on the street by an intoxicated man shouting anti-Jewish obscenities, Eduard was there at her defense, and calming the demonically irate comrade.

Yelena, also a Bible School student, though reserved and quiet, proved steadfast and faithful all week long. When we drew her out of her shell, we found a depth of character, insight and maturity far beyond her twenty-two years.

Yelena had come to the Lord three years earlier, after a long and despairing search for the meaning of life. Yeshua revealed Himself to her, she said, in a vision, then gave her a burden for the Jewish people. Normally demure and unanimated, Yelena witnessed on the streets of Moscow with a gentle boldness and unpretentious tenacity not uncommon among Russian believers. "I know now that I am called to be an evangelist," she said at the end of the week, without any discernible trace of pride.

Ilvira was even quieter but no less persevering than Yelena. In her late twenties, Ilvira had been a believer for five years. One of her parents was Jewish, and the other, Russian. To spare her the hardships of anti-Semitism, they had secured a passport identifying her as Russian. Documents notwithstanding, when Yeshua came into her life, He quickened to her spirit her Jewish identity.

Immediately, Ilvira tried to join the synagogue in St. Petersburg but was refused because of her passport. Then she tried, unsuccessfully, to find a church that embraced its Jewish heritage. It wasn't until the St. Petersburg festival two years earlier that she found others of similar vision and heart. Ilvira has been a committed member of the Messianic congregation ever since. Like Yelena, she feels called to a life-long labor for the Jewish people.

Our team translator was a twenty-two-year-old Ukrainian college student named Olga. Olga had previously interpreted for us in Kiev, and we loved her as if she were our own little sister. Also somewhat of an introvert, Olga came vibrantly alive at any opportunity to love the lost.

Olga's only fault, if it could be counted as one, was her tendency to succumb to the Spirit and quit translating in the middle of a conversation. An unstoppable stream of Russian would erupt and, before long, she would gently take the hand of whoever we were speaking with and introduce them to Jesus. When it was all over, she would remember English. . .and meekly apologize.

The ways of the world seemed to have little hold on Olga—or Eduard, Yelena or Ilvira. Theirs is a simpler and purer, if not an easier, life in many respects. Olga, for instance, lives with her parents in a small flat, as do most young people in the CIS. Her parents are staunch Communists and atheists. They are adamantly opposed to her faith. Through her struggle to lovingly submit to them, she has learned to lean on the Lord to a depth not often required of those her age in the West. When she wasn't translating, ministering or joking, she was certain to be worshipping or praying quietly under her breath.

One time we confided in Olga how difficult it was for us to minister in a foreign city, fall in love with the people, then leave after a few days, never to see them again. "It feels like we keep giving away pieces of our hearts," Scott said. "When we go home, those pieces stay here. It gets harder to do because it feels like we have fewer pieces left to give."

Olga understood, and was quick with the solution. "Then we must ask God to make our hearts bigger," she offered reassuringly.

She must have followed her own advice; whenever anyone on the team needed encouragement or a kind word, Olga seemed to be there with it. She always had a piece of her heart for those in need.

Olga had a friend named Alex, a classmate, who was also on our team and who we also first met in Kiev. If Olga was always praying or singing, Alex was perpetually reading his Bible every spare moment he could find. His one and only copy of the Scriptures had gotten so worn out in the four years he'd known the Lord that, by the time we were in Moscow, it was precariously held together by string, tape and rubber bands. A whole section dropped out of it one day while he caught a few minutes' reading time on the Metro. He laughed and shrugged his shoulders when Olga interrupted his subway study to retrieve the fly-away pages before the next stop. Alex demonstrated a carefree yet focused enjoyment of the Lord that provoked us to jealousy.

Scott and I had tried to give Alex some money in Kiev but he wouldn't take it. We were leaving the country the next day and wouldn't be allowed to take Ukrainian currency with us. Changing it back to dollars wasn't easy; it seemed much better just to leave whatever we had with our brothers and sisters. We remembered that Alex had worn the same clothes almost every day and had been chronically late because he didn't own a watch. In Ukraine, the equivalent of twenty dollars could buy a month's groceries, a couple of pairs of shoes, a quality watch or a new Bible, but Alex couldn't be persuaded. The twenty dollars we offered was a huge sum, he said, and he didn't need it. He already had a good pair of shoes, enough food to eat and a Bible. A watch he had long done without, which only proved he didn't need one.

Alex's protestations didn't stem from pride. He really didn't need anything—and had the rare sense to know it. We shouldn't worry about him, he said. Jesus said He would provide what we need, and He did this for Alex. He had his clothes, his pair of shoes, his food, his strung-together Bible, and his bed in his parents' flat.

Eventually Alex agreed to take the money because he knew a family of believers that was really poor. "They can never buy chicken or meat and they are all really skinny. I will give it to them."

In contrast to these gentle and sweet, yet bold and steadfastly dedicated believers are the many others who could be described as forthright and fiery, intensely and unstoppably zealous. Such a one was on our team—which is about the right number for any small group!

Nikolai, another of the Bible school students, saw every soul on the streets of Moscow as possibly entering judgment's gates that day. It was therefore *imperative* that he witness to whoever the Lord allowed to cross his path—or, more, accurately, field of vision. More than once we had to tell Nikolai to stop running after people in the streets. Often he would chase them for blocks just to make sure they had a festival invitation and the opportunity to hear the gospel. On every evangelistic outing, long-legged Nikolai was the first to run out of invitations and return to us, panting and perspiring, for more.

Nikolai was not unlike a Russian Jewish believer named Gleb who had been on our team the year before in Moscow and Minsk. Gleb was a nineteen-year-old ex-con who'd met Jesus two years before he met us. He'd just made aliyah with his mother a few weeks ago, we were told. But before he left Russia, he'd managed to launch a successful prison ministry in the Moscow jails.

Like Nikolai, Gleb was a fireball and extremely articulate. His square, wide-jawed face was set like flint for the purposes of God. Gleb, however, prayed more and chased less. Since people for whom Gleb prayed often got instantly healed of medical conditions, this young brother had led hundreds of Russians to the Lord before leaving for Israel. An outing with Gleb was inevitably an encounter with the miraculous. (We later learned that, within a year of his arrival, Gleb started a Russian Messianic congregation in Israel.)

The boundless energy and enthusiasm of these foot soldiers was matched by a similar devotion and passion in the Russian intercessors who came to participate in the outreach. The majority were middle-aged women enrolled in prayer classes at the Messianic Bible school. Day and night, these faithful ones cried out to the Lord from the very depths of their souls.

The prayer room set up for the festival was always open, so anyone on the outreach could participate in whatever intercessory watch happened to be in progress. In addition, the intercessors welcomed the opportunity to pray over the evangelists and administrators. Consequently, I made time for the prayer room on every outreach, either to participate in a watch or ask for prayer. In either case, it was bound to be an adventure.

I first visited the prayer room during last year's outreach in Moscow. I was suffering from a serious bout with bronchitis and every breath I took hurt my chest. Prayer, I knew, could only help. Unfortunately the intercessors didn't speak English, and often they had no interpreter. But I decided to take my chances. I walked into the room and sheepishly pointed at my throat and chest and made "ouch" faces and sounds. They nodded and smiled, as if to let me know they understood.

The next thing I knew, I was surrounded by a dozen very emotional, grandmotherly ladies, none of whom I knew, weeping all over me and covering me with kisses. A few minutes later, they started wailing. Their prayers were very loud.

A perplexing burst of histrionics followed. All I had, I thought amidst the wailing, shouting and sobbing, was a sore throat and chest congestion. Maybe they didn't understand the prayer request. Or, worse yet, maybe they *did*. . . and I was a lot worse off than I thought.

In any event, I knew they wouldn't stop until they obtained the desired result. These ladies were determined. They would stay put at the throne of grace, pouring their hearts out like the widow before the unjust judge in Luke 18. . .*on my behalf*! Suddenly I felt *very* ashamed of my pride.

A few minutes later, I began to sense the distinct presence of God. Another few minutes and my chest felt very hot—until it stopped hurting altogether. I looked at these precious sisters with tears running down their cheeks. They didn't even know my name. It was terribly humbling.

"They always pray like that," said one of the American intercessors who walked into the room towards the end of the wailing. "It doesn't matter that they don't know you. They really love you. That's just how they are."

✧ ✧ ✧ ✧

God has honored the humble cries and zealous faith of our Russian brothers and sisters. In His hand, the desolate soil of the former Soviet Union has become fertile spiritual breeding ground. Many have been the children of these heretofore barren ones, these believers both old and new. God has "enlarged the place of their tent," "stretched out" and "expanded" them "to the right and to the left."

Our mandate to equip and release the ministry to our indigenous Russian counterparts was indisputably confirmed the first night of the festival. Not quite an hour into the concert, militiamen with semi-automatic weapons stormed the stadium, putting an abrupt end to the program.

The team leaders, posted as watchmen at different sectors around the stadium, were the first to see them come. A bewildered walkie-talkie communiqué with those of us inside followed. Nobody knew why the police were there or what would happen once they got inside the building.

After what felt like an hour but was only a minute, an announcement came over the public address system: "By order of the Moscow police, everyone must evacuate the stadium immediately. We have a bomb threat."

Most of the team instantly perceived it to be a hoax, probably because we had faced threats of violence, some of them rather formidable, in the past. For the same reason, however, others took the matter more seriously. We knew we had enemies. In previous cities there had been brushes with bomb threats. Someday it could in fact happen. . .

In any event, it seemed to all of us at that moment in Moscow that the opposition had finally found a way to stop us. Several thousand guests inside the stadium solemnly gathered their belongings and left for home. As we watched them go, we grew indignant. These people had come to hear the good news of Jesus Christ. The Lord would never have sent them away like this.

Most of us promptly started sharing about Messiah with whomever we could find. Soon small crowds gathered all around the stadium. The musicians ministered as best they could in the parking lot. Jonathan himself refused to leave the scene. He had come to preach the gospel and wouldn't leave until he did. Despite the disruption, many hundreds heard about Yeshua and made professions of faith. And by the end of the evening, the police determined there had, after all, been no bomb.

To our surprise the concert guests were unfazed. "It happens here in Moscow all the time," they said. "We will come back tomorrow." That only gave us cause for further concern, however. The police said they'd received an anonymous phone call warning them about a bomb set to go off. Whether this call had come from anti-missionaries, neofascists, Communists, ultra-nationalists, the Russian Mafia or someone else, it had successfully put an end to the festival. In all likelihood, the persons responsible would try again. We decided that if they did,

Jonathan, who had been getting death threats for quite some time, would get whisked away while the rest of us reorganized the meeting outdoors.

The following night, as if right on cue, the militia streamed into the stadium, announcing another evacuation for another bomb search. With all the hospitality and grace we could muster, we escorted our guests outside and tried to resume the concert. Though many stayed, most did not. Our team was disheartened. What was wrong?

The next day we canceled all outreach activities and called for team-wide prayer and fasting. We were in a battle we didn't know how to fight. God, so it seemed, was silent. All we could do was get down on our faces, to seek only His.

We were so pathetically few in number that we regularly encouraged each other with the story of Gideon's army. Nonetheless, had we given way to pride and presumption? Or were we just encountering the unavoidable realities of missionary work in an unstable land?

We left for the final concert hoping for the best but prepared for the worst. We had an outdoor stage erected next to the stadium so that, if necessary, we could "move the party to the terrace." Predictably, by mid-concert we were on the "terrace" while Moscow's bomb squad searched the stadium for a third night in a row.

All we ever learned from the police was that the bomb threats had been called in each evening from different phone booths around the city. Nobody ever claimed responsibility.

The situation did not change when we left for St. Petersburg the next week. Our first concert was cut short by the now all-too-familiar bomb scare and evacuation. So once more, we scrapped our agenda and dedicated most of each day to prayer. Our work, the battle plans, the salvation of souls, all seemed to come to a halt.

Finally, things turned around. Mindful of the past week's track record of false alarms in Moscow, the concert hall director refused to let the militia force an evacuation the second night until after Jonathan's salvation message. Then, the third night, there was no bomb threat at all. We knew from Whom the victory had come.

We were sobered but grateful. The bomb threats could have been, and may someday be, real. Were we ready for that eventuality? Were we willing to lay our lives down for the sake of the gospel?

The apparent defeat we faced in Russia in the spring of 1995 left the ministry walking, in a sense, with a limp. But like the dislocation of Jacob's thigh, our disjointed mission would hopefully remind us forever of our absolute dependence on the Lord.

The doors were beginning to close for us in Russia—but only to open wider for the indigenous believers. It was time, and they were ready, for *their* tents to expand. Our Russian brothers and sisters were rising to new levels of maturity, responsibility and spiritual authority. We would give them all we could for the task, for as long as we could. Then we would entrust them to the Lord. We knew He would not disappoint them—nor they, Him.

Odessa: Restoration to the Land

"This is what the Lord says; 'Sing with joy for Jacob; shout for the foremost of the nations. Make your praises heard and say, "O Lord, save Your people, the remnant of Israel." See, I will bring them from the Land of the North and gather them from the ends of the earth. Among them will be the blind and the lame, expectant mothers and women in labor; a great throng will return. They will come with weeping; they will pray as I bring them back. I will lead them beside streams of water, on a level path where they will not stumble, because I am Israel's Father, and Ephraim is My firstborn son. Hear the word of the Lord, O nations; proclaim it in distant coastlands: "He who scattered Israel will gather them and will watch over His flock like a shepherd."'"

Jeremiah 31:7-10

AT THE END OF THE NINETEENTH CENTURY, study circles and clubs promoting emigration to Palestine began to spring up in different cities throughout Russia's Pale of Settlement.[87] Known collectively as *Hovevei Zion* (Hebrew for "Lovers of Zion"), these groups gave rise to modern-day Zionism,[88] i.e., the re-establishment of a Jewish State in Palestine. Their credo was that there was no salvation for the Jewish people apart from their regathering in the land of Israel.[89] Centuries of persecution in the Land of the North had made this painfully clear.

The Zionist movement gained great impetus in 1882 after a wave of pogroms and the passage of anti-Jewish laws by Czar Alexander III. The czar justified these laws on religious grounds. "We must not forget," he said, "that it was the Jews who crucified our Lord and spilled His priceless blood."[90]

In the wake of renewed anti-Semitism, Hovevei Zion organized and located its central offices in the seaport city of Odessa (now in Ukraine). One of Hovevei Zion's main goals was to support and direct emigration for the establishment of Jewish agricultural colonies in Palestine. [91] Since Odessa was on the Black Sea, it provided a strategic vantage point for aliyah. Thus the city served as Russian Zionism's main center of activity until World War I.[92] From Odessa were issued the first calls for "the revival of Israel in the land of its ancestors."[93] The city became known as Russia's "Gateway to Zion."[94]

Out of Odessa's harbors sailed steamships boarded by zealous, young Jewish pioneers.[95] These hard-working idealists were determined to reclaim and restore the swamps and deserts in the land of their fathers. Among the Odessan seafarers was a young man named David Ben-Gurion.[96] Some forty years later, as Israel's first prime minister, Ben-Gurion would officially proclaim the independence of the Jewish State and the "right of the Jewish people to a national revival in their own country."[97]

The early Hovevei Zion visionaries linked a return to Israel with the coming of Messiah and the dawn of their redemption.[98] The movement soon became secularized, however, and, by the turn of the century, its focus had shifted to ensuring the survival of the Jewish people.[99] Nonetheless, some of the founding fathers had caught a genuine prophetic glimpse from the Word of God.

Decades before modern-day Zionism took root, small pockets of fundamentalist Christians in England and the United States were praying and calling for a return of the Jews to their biblical homeland. [100] "Christian Zionism" was largely the result of a fresh emphasis in the mid-nineteenth century on the literal interpretation of the Scriptures. Prophecies concerning the land of Israel were understood as referring specifically to ethnic Jews. Those passages were not, according to emerging theologians like John Darby, to be spiritualized away or applied in totality to the church.[101]

These nineteenth century fundamentalists based their Zionist claims to the land on the Abrahamic covenant.[102] In Genesis 12:7, after Abraham arrived in Canaan, God said to him, "To your offspring I will give this land." This unconditional promise was repeated throughout the patriarchal period and thereafter. [103] It was specifically and exclusively applied to Isaac and his descendants—but not Ishmael—in Genesis 17:18-21, 26:3-4 and 28:13. The Old Testament prophets, even during the exile, reaffirmed God's covenant concerning the land. They foretold a return to the land following both the exile at hand and a future worldwide dispersion. [104] In the New Testament, nowhere is the land covenant canceled out. [105]

The nineteenth century Christian Zionists trace their roots to the publication of the King James Bible in 1611. By the mid 1600's, Puritan theologians began to interpret the Scriptures literally, as opposed to allegorically. Thus, they saw the Jews as a people, and Israel as a land, with a definite destiny. They understood that the Jews' return to Israel was connected to the return of the Lord, and His rule and reign on the earth. [106]

Admittedly, the Puritans were motivated less by a love for the Jews than by zeal for the fulfillment of prophecy. [107] Nonetheless, they were a force to be reckoned with. In 1649 they petitioned the British government: "That this Nation of England, with the inhabitants of the Netherlands, shall be the first and the readiest to transport Izraell's sons and daughters in their ships to the Land promised their forefathers, Abraham, Isaac and Jacob, for an everlasting inheritance."[108] Although these believers' commendable efforts did not take hold, seeds were planted that would sprout at a later date.

In the 1700's, rationalism overtook religion and pro-Zionist theology subsided. But in the mid-1800's it re-emerged in the larger context of an evangelical revival in England. [109] Christian Zionism, as it developed from that time forward, proved indispensable to the success of the aliyah movement. From English Christians came practical help with emigration, as well as financial, political and behind-the-scenes military assistance. [110]

Lord Antony Ashley Cooper, Earl of Shaftesbury, was one of aliyah's earliest Christian supporters. He took the lead in the mid-1800's in combining religious fervor with political action. He tirelessly wrote, lectured and met with political heads of state for the sake of promoting Jewish nationhood. "Pray for the peace of Jerusalem," was engraved on the ring he wore on his right hand.[111]

Laurence Oliphant, an officer in the British Foreign Service and member of Parliament, fervently pleaded the cause of the Jews' restoration to Palestine. Oliphant was especially concerned for Russian Jews who were subject to a rising wave of anti-Semitism in the form of pogroms. He garnered some measure of support from England, France, Wales and Schleswig-Holstein. In 1879, Oliphant traveled to Palestine, trying to devise a plan by which he might implement the prophesied return of God's people to their land.[112]

Lending spiritual support and counsel to the aliyah movement was the Rev. William Hechler, chaplain of the British Embassy in Vienna. Hechler challenged fellow Christian Zionists to sincerely love the Jews—not merely to esteem them as prophetic timepieces.[113] He worked closely for many years with Theodor Herzl, the Austrian Jew hailed as the founding father of the Jewish State. "According to the Bible," Hechler declared, "The Jews must return to Palestine and I, therefore, must help this movement as a Christian, and in complete faith in the truth of the Bible. For this is the cause of God."[114]

In the United States, the most vocal proponent of aliyah was a fundamentalist Methodist minister in Chicago named William Blackstone. In 1878 Blackstone authored the book "Jesus is Coming," calling for the restoration of Israel.[115] By the turn of the century, Blackstone managed to bring the issue of mass Jewish settlement in Palestine to the attention of the American public and US government.[116] He was especially concerned about anti-Semitism in Russia, and prophetically foresaw the Holocaust which he said it heralded.[117]

Other American Christian sympathizers, such as Charles Russell, preached the Zionist cause from a biblical perspective not only to political groups, but to the American Jewish community as well. Russell taught that the Jews' return to Israel would culminate in their salvation as a nation and untold blessing to all humanity.[118] By the onset of World War II, the most vigorous assistance and open support of Zionism came from Christian groups in the United States.[119]

The Scriptures foretold the Gentiles would play a key role in the restoration of the Jews to their land. Concerning the regathering of the nation of Israel, Isaiah wrote: "This is what the Sovereign Lord says: 'See, I will beckon to the Gentiles, I will lift up My banner to the peoples; they will bring your sons in their arms and carry your daughters on their shoulders.'" (Isaiah 49:22)[120]

✧　✧　✧　✧

At the Messianic Jewish Festival in Odessa in August 1994, the Lord's "beckon to the Gentiles" sounded with richly historic reverberation. A hundred years ago, the city and its seaport had served as Russia's gateway to Zion for thousands of emigrants. But millions of Jews still remained in the former Soviet Union.[121] The Lord had shown some of the intercessors the importance in His plan of the Black Sea harbor gates reopening toward Zion. Perhaps this might relate to a future season of renewed anti-Semitism, when exit visas and airplanes wouldn't be as available as they were now. . .

When we arrived in Odessa, things concerning the festival seemed surprisingly calm. In contrast to our recent undertakings in Moscow and St. Petersburg, we sensed an unusual but most welcome presence of grace and peace. In fact, this outreach would actually unfold without any major opposition—at least in the natural realm.

Most of us dismissed the prediction of ease that came at our first corporate prayer meeting, where a team member spoke prophetically. "There will be a tremendous outpouring of the Holy Spirit here," he said, "with signs and wonders following. God's glory will be made known in this place. There will be no opposition. He has already won the victory! There will be healings as we preach the Word. The heavens will be opened. Rejoice! You will freely harvest this time. There will not be opposition."

Carol, the director of intercession, believed the prophecy. It was consistent with the Lord's prayer assignment for us that week. She knew that this time we were not to intercede exclusively for the outreach and its follow-up.

"First Corinthians 10:1-2 states that when the children of Israel left Egypt, they were under a cloud as they passed through the sea," Carol said. "The Lord showed me that multitudes of Jews are yet to leave the former Soviet Union. When they do, they too will be under a cloud and many will pass through by way of the sea. The Lord wants to direct and use our prayers this week to form a cloud covering over the Black Sea in the exodus of Jews yet to come."

Carol jumped with excitement as she spoke, her emerald green eyes twinkling. "We will pray for the outreach," she continued, "and the salvation of the people of Odessa. But our vision in this city must be broader than just the festival. This city is unique because it is strategic in God's end-time purposes for the Jewish people. His restoration of Israel is on two related levels: spiritual and physical. We will be concerned with Israel's spiritual restoration as we pray for salvations and the festival. But we will also be concerned with Israel's *physical* restoration as we focus our prayers on the exodus to come."

I was especially glad after listening to Carol that on this outreach I'd signed up to serve in intercession. And despite my tendency toward seasickness, the next I knew I was on a boat with a dozen other intercessors, riding the Black Sea and praying up a cloud. We had rented a small, sputtering, Soviet-era tour vessel for the morning. It provided a perfect platform from which to worship God, pray over the water and proclaim the release of the Jews from the Land of the North.

The old Black Sea route to Israel had been discontinued in 1941.[122] By the 1950's, it was virtually impossible to escape the USSR through the Port of Odessa. The Communists were extremely strict with passenger control on every boat.[123] But recently, a Christian Zionist from England had had a vision to "bring Israel's sons on his arms and carry her daughters on his shoulders" by boat from Odessa again.

In 1991, Gustav Scheller established a shipping line to Haifa and, since then, has carried over 10,000 former Soviet Jews to Israel.[124] En route, the emigrants are exposed to the love of Christ (although, due to the ministry's agreement with the State of Israel, there is no proselytizing). The ministry hopes to keep its line available and running in the event of increased persecution of the Jews in the CIS. Some of the intercessors at the festival visited Scheller's dock in Odessa and prayed a cloud covering over his ship . . .

The Bible teaches that, as Jews exiled around the world turn back to God, He will restore them to the Land. Thus their spiritual restoration *precedes* their physical restoration:

> "When all these blessings and curses I have set before you come upon you and you take them to heart wherever the Lord your God disperses you among the nations, and when you and your children return to the Lord your God and obey Him with all your heart and with all your soul according to everything I command you today, then the Lord your God will restore your fortunes and have compassion on you and gather you again from all the nations where He scattered you. Even if you have been banished to the most distant land under the heavens, from there the Lord your God will gather you and bring you back. He will bring you to the land that belonged to your fathers and you will take possession of it." (Deuteronomy 30:1-5; see also, Nehemiah 1:8-9)

Based on the Scriptures, our vision is that, as Jews in the CIS first turn to their Messiah—the only way to "obey Him with all your heart"—they will return to Israel as spiritual pioneers, bearing seeds of revival. (Thus the pastors of the congregation birthed from the Odessa festival named their fellowship "Gateway to Zion." But they had no inkling, they say, of the past significance of that name in this city.)

At the same time, there is biblical support for the physical restoration of Israel taking place before the Jewish people turn to Christ.[125] Different theological explanations have been offered for the apparent anomaly. Some even see two modern-day regatherings in the Land, the first to bring Israel to repentance, the second to usher in the Lord's return.

In any event, the reality is that God seems to be doing it both ways. He has begun to regather Israel while the people remain, for the most part, in unbelief. At the same time, more Jews have turned to Yeshua in the latter half of the 20th century than at any other time since the start of the New Testament church. While the overwhelming majority of these recent converts do not live in Israel, increasing numbers are making aliyah.

Christian Zionists have long labored under the belief that God would first physically restore Israel, then sovereignly deal with her spiritually. A full fifty years have passed since Israel's restored nationhood. In the wake of her Year of Jubilee,[126] may Christians who hold to this belief remain steadfast in prayer for the spiritual restoration of those who returned in unbelief . . .

In the meantime, Yeshua said He did what He saw the Father doing. We wanted to do the same. We wanted to bless the prophetic ministry of the modern-day Christian Zionists. We could not predict precisely how the Lord would work in the years ahead but we knew the physical and spiritual were intimately tied together.

We also believed that the spiritual forces holding the Jews in physical bondage in the former Soviet Union were much the same as would keep them in bondage spiritually. Could these even be similar to those enemies the children of Israel had faced 3,400 years ago when they lived in Egypt, in bondage to a Pharaoh who would not let them go?

There were reasons to suspect this could be so. First, the Bible says that the exodus beginning from the Land of the North will call to mind and even outweigh the ancient deliverance from the hand of Pharaoh: "The days are coming," declares the Lord, "when men will no longer say, 'As surely as the Lord lives, who brought the Israelites up out of Egypt,' but they will say, 'As surely as the Lord lives, who brought the Israelites up out of the land of the north. . .'" (Jeremiah 16:14-15)

Second, interesting parallels belie Egypt and the former Soviet Union vis-à-vis the Jewish people. The Scriptures describe Egypt as that place where the Jews wrongly turned for help, instead of turning to God.[127] This was especially detestable because Egypt was a blatantly idolatrous nation. The Pharaoh was reckoned among the gods and regarded as their representative on earth.[128] Of course, to the children of Israel, he became a paranoid taskmaster.

Historians believe the Jews first arrived in the region of the former Soviet Union during the Babylonian exile of 586 BC. The earliest Jewish communities were probably founded on the northern shores of the Black Sea, not far from Odessa. They were established mainly for purposes of commercial trade. The area, so it seemed, provided a safe harbor for the dispersed Jews.[129] But the rulers of this region were worshipped as demi-gods. First with the advent of Russian Orthodoxy, then with Communism, religion and government mixed together and formed a territorial stronghold. Russia's early princes were deemed the representatives of God's kingdom on earth— which happened to be located in Russia. The political theory was that the czar could do no wrong and was accountable only to God.[130]

With the advent of Communism, and despite its official atheistic stance, Lenin, more or less, replaced the czar as the national object of veneration. Interestingly, his remains were embalmed and enshrined in Red Square, somewhat reminiscent of the ancient Egyptian burial rite. And like the Pharaohs, under the rubric of the socialist work ethic, the Communist leaders proved to be harsh taskmasters. Neither would they let the Jews who wanted to leave, go.

God declared that He would be the One to judge Pharaoh and his hordes. For their idolatry, He would make the land of Egypt desolate. Then, He said, they would know that He was the Lord.[131] Too weakened to rule over other peoples, Egypt would serve as a reminder of Israel's sin in turning to that nation for help. (Ezekiel 29:15-16)

Similarly, has God been the One to judge Russia and its hordes of the former Soviet Union? Has He been the One to render its land desolate, its rulers too weakened to rule over other peoples as they once did? Has He been the One to demonstrate to multitudes of disillusioned ex-Soviet Jews the folly of placing hope in any nation's supposed safe harbor?. . .

A statue of Pharaoh overlooks Odessa's seaport. Behind the Pharaoh stands a nine-foot-high carving of an Egyptian cobra. (According to Egyptian mythology, the cobra-god served as an important and protective source of the Pharaohs' power.[132]) The statues are located on top of and behind an old wooden structure that is now a pool hall. The pool hall is near the stadium where the Messianic festival was to be held. Pharaoh and his cobra are relatively hidden from sight, but they were discovered by the intercessors who went out to spiritually map the city. The mappers also learned from the locals that Jews caught trying to flee the former Soviet Union by way of the sea were taken into this same wooden building and shot.

The idols, if that was what they were, certainly had no power. But could they attract and represent real demonic forces? Were these images actually intended to serve as a type of *Baal Zephon*, which, meaning "lord of the north,"[133] was the place where the children of Israel crossed the sea as they left Egypt and were overtaken by Pharaoh? (Exodus 14:1-9) Or was Pharaoh's presence merely a coincidence?

The intercessors took the entire outreach team on a prayer-walk past the stadium, pool hall, and harbor before the festival began. Given the Lord's strategic purposes for the city, we wanted to pray as a whole group at these key locations for the release of the former Soviet Jews.

As we filed past the pool hall and peeked in an open door, I was struck by the darkness inside. Such darkness could almost be felt, perhaps not unlike the plague that once struck Egypt. I couldn't help but notice that Pharaoh rested on a pedestal and that, under his feet, which looked a bit like bear's claws, were four billiard balls. The balls were numbered 1, 6, 9 and 13. It was a bizarre hodgepodge.

It has been said that in the Bible, different numbers have different representative meanings. The particular numbers on the billiard balls under the Pharaoh have been thought to represent: (1) beginnings; (6) man; (9) judgment; and (13) rebellion.[134] Of course the symbolism is speculative, but it still seemed an ill-intentioned combination.

The team gathered on a grassy knoll overlooking the harbor, a good distance from the pool hall. Beneath us, freighters and motorboats criss-crossed calm, sapphire sea waters. We wanted to pray with wisdom. We would not rail accusations at the Pharaoh or proceed to knock him off his pedestal. The Bible says God Himself will deal with Pharaoh and his hordes. If such were the spiritual forces involved, we would leave them to face Him. If, on the other hand, we were being over-imaginative, and Pharoah had no part in the matter, why waste our time on senseless prayers? Thus we focused our petitions on the deliverance of God's people from bondage. "Let Your people go into their destiny!" we cried over and again.

A Gentile believer from Odessa beseeched God for forgiveness. "We have mistreated the Jewish people," he cried. "We did not try to help them go. We have only hated them."

A Messianic Jew whose grandfather had emigrated to the US from Odessa responded. "Extend Your forgiveness to this city, Lord. Have mercy and do not hold their sin against them. Bless them with the power of salvation."

A second Messianic Jew in the group stepped forward. "Forgive us, too, Lord, for we are not without fault. We have sinned against You and the nations by not following You. We, too, have worshipped idols. Only You can strike down our enemies. Would you part the waters of our hearts this week? Open the gates of our souls. Then send Your Spirit to part the waters of the sea and open wide the gates to Zion!"

By now, twilight had fallen. We turned on our flashlights and prayed specifically for the concerts, unctioned by Jeremiah 31: 7: "Sing with joy for Jacob; shout for the foremost of the nations. Make your praises heard and say, 'O Lord, save your people, the remnant of Israel.'"

The Lord's response—aliyah—follows in the next two verses: "See, *I will bring them from the Land of the North* and gather them from the ends of the earth. Among them will be the blind and the lame, expectant mothers and women in labor; a great throng will return. They will come with weeping; *they will pray as I bring them back.* I will lead them beside streams of water on a level path where they will not stumble, because I am Israel's father, and Ephraim is My firstborn son." (Jeremiah 31:8-9, emphases added.)

Then we proclaimed what the next verse instructs, the restoration of Israel: "Hear the word of the Lord, O nations; *proclaim it in distant coastlands.* 'He who scattered Israel will gather them and will watch over His flock like a shepherd.'" (Jeremiah 31:10, emphasis added)

Our prayer-walk continued into the outdoor, Olympic-size soccer stadium where the festival would be held. Up and down the dilapidated rows of 40,000 seats we walked and prayed, and walked and prayed. By the time we assembled in the center of the arena to leave, our feet throbbing, it was quite late. The majority of the group had already gone back to the hotel. But that was when those of us who were left, saw the cloud appear.

It drifted slowly into the stadium from the inland side, *against* the coastal breeze. A third of the stadium's length and punctuated by tall floodlights, the puffy white cloud contrasted sharply against the night sky. What was most odd, however, was that it settled right into the stadium and hovered no more than a hundred feet above ground.

"Look," shouted one of the intercessors, "the glory cloud!"

Within seconds, everyone's eyes were glued to the cloud. We were positively transfixed. I'd never seen anything like it. Nonetheless, while all those around me were confident it was a supernatural sign from heaven, I was sure it was an optical illusion.

"It's the cloud of prayer!" shrieked a friend of mine.

"It's the exodus cloud!" uttered another, tears running down her face.

I waited for evidence to appear that would rationally explain the cloud's extraordinary form and arrival. Probably it was smoke belched from some timeworn apparatus nearby, or the beginning of a frontal system moving in. But I could find no evidence to back my theories. In the meantime, the cloud hovered overhead for several minutes. Then, just as gradually as it had moved in, it dissipated and drifted out to sea. I was forced to the same belated conclusion as my more trusting colleagues. It seemed a supernatural manifestation, some sort of cloud of God's presence.

In both the Old and New Testaments, God's manifest presence is associated with clouds. After the exodus from Egypt, the children of Israel were instructed to follow the cloud of His glory all the way to the Promised Land. Was there prophetic symbolism in the stadium cloud that drifted out to sea? And what of its settling temporarily right in the stadium? After the tabernacle was erected in the wilderness, a cloud covered and settled upon the tent of meeting. Then the glory of the Lord filled the tabernacle and fire was there by night. (Exodus 40: 33-38) The cloud was, it turned out, only the first of a host of signs and wonders to manifest in the stadium, our tabernacle for the week. Fire would indeed appear there by night!

✧ ✧ ✧ ✧

The sheer magnitude of the stadium concert overwhelmed us all. About 60,000 people came to the concerts, half of whom were Jewish.

At least 45,000 stood to repent of their sins and commit their lives to Yeshua. The stadium director insisted that 80,000 people had attended. One of his deputies said he'd never seen the place so full. It was the first time since the onset of Communism, the director remarked, that Jews in Odessa had openly celebrated their heritage.

We held a buffet reception the second night of the festival to honor the local Holocaust survivors. Afterwards, we seated them in the grandstand VIP booth for the concert. Eager to get to know some of these noble ones, I sat down among them for the evening. They seemed to enjoy the praise and worship. When Jonathan gave the invitation for salvation, all the survivors around me rose to their feet to pray. Overcome with emotion, I strained to hear each word they repeated and watched peace descend on their faces. But I was too close to the fire to see it.

Shortly before the sinner's prayer, several team members said they spotted a flaming red ball in the sky over the stadium. It floated, they insisted, slowly over to the VIP booth. There it stopped and rested directly in front of the Holocaust survivors. After several minutes, it faded away. The testimonies of those who observed the fireball all matched. These eyewitnesses were so excited and articulate about what they'd seen, I could not discount them.

After the prayer of repentance, Jonathan invited people to stand who needed physical healing. "God wants to touch some of you here and heal you," he announced. "It has nothing to do with any power I have. It has everything to do with God's power and love for you. So if you are sick, please stand up."

Almost as many people as had stood for salvation stood throughout the stadium for physical healing. As best I could see, not one Holocaust survivor remained seated. I didn't doubt the sincerity of their response. I had been visiting hospitals and talking to doctors all week long (in between prayer-walks). Disease ran rampant in the Odessa region.

"In the name of Messiah," Jonathan began, "I pray for everyone standing tonight. I ask, Father, for Your healing power to flow through this stadium. Restore the bodies of all who are sick. Thank you for Your mercy."

It was a simple prayer, noticeably lacking in emotional hype or promises. But reports of dramatic and instantaneous healings soon echoed from ecstatic folks all over the stadium.

The next night, Jonathan repeated the prayer for healing, instructing team members to follow-up during the altar ministry. The results were astounding. Several claimed they were healed of deafness. A cross-eyed child was healed, his eyes literally straightening out that night. A man rendered mute from a diseased larynx gained back his speech. An excited usher from one of the local churches grabbed Jonathan after the concert to tell him about a woman who had come to the festival with a severe hip malady, hobbling on crutches. The woman was still running around the stadium, leaping and praising God when Jonathan heard the story. Testimonies of healed head and back ailments poured in. People reported the relief of pain for several other, more internal conditions not so visibly measurable, but nonetheless serious. Although circumstances did not allow for medical documentation, the majority of team members reported personally witnessing someone get instantly healed in Odessa. " 'I will restore you to health and heal your wounds,' declares the Lord, 'because you are called an outcast, Zion for whom no one cares.'" (Jeremiah 30:17)

Mindful of the Lord's desire to heal, we had already dispatched over three tons of medical aid to Odessa via shipping container before leaving the States. In addition, we brought with us medicine, vitamins and clothing for orphans and Holocaust survivors—all desperately needed. Disease had ravaged this city. Poverty was widespread. Community hygiene was nonexistent by Western standards. Much of the population was malnourished. The water supply was contaminated. The people who worked, worked hard—and sometimes without pay, since the government regularly ran out of money. How could we preach the love of Christ in such circumstances without extending His compassion in a practical way?

Those who received humanitarian aid were effusively thankful. Many wept as they realized the Lord had neither forgotten nor forsaken them. It was in this context that Scott and I met Leonid, the stoic president of the local Holocaust survivors association, as well as Liena, the sweet, abandoned child at the orphanage. We did all we humanly could for them.

But Leonid did not release his life to his Messiah, and the Ukrainian government did not release Liena. So we continue to join in the cry of the Spirit on their behalf, "Let My people go!"

We remain hopeful for the Leonids and Lienas of Odessa and the rest of the former Soviet Union, for we have seen a cloud. The glory of God has begun to return to Israel. Maybe that cloud is only "as small as a man's hand." (I Kings 18:44) But out of the darkness, on the distant northern horizon, it has most definitely appeared.

"For Zion's sake I will not keep silent, for Jerusalem's sake I will not remain quiet, till her righteousness shines out like the dawn, her salvation like a blazing torch. The nations will see your righteousness, and all kings your glory; you will be called by a new name that the mouth of the Lord will bestow."

Isaiah 62: 1-2

8

Epilogue:

Understanding the Times

"And the sons of Issachar [were] men who understood the times, with knowledge of what Israel should do...."

I Chronicles 12:32, NAS

FIRST CHRONICLES RECOUNTS THAT DAVID, son of Jesse, had set up camp at Hebron, when so many men came to join him that soon he had a battle force like the army of God. The Israelites who aligned with David had determined to crown him king. David's fame had spread throughout the land. Saul had fallen in battle. It was time to turn the kingdom over to him, as the Lord had said.

Among those who joined forces with David were many men from the clan of Issachar. These were men of wisdom, the Bible says, who understood the times and knew what Israel should do. (I Chronicles 12:32) The first thing they wanted to do under King David's rule was retrieve the ark of God, or restore God's presence to Israel. (I Chronicles 13:1-4)

The sons and daughters of Issachar are just as important to God's purposes today as they were 3,000 years ago. Jesus instructs us to watch and pray always. He urges us to understand the times, that we might know how best to redeem them. He tells us to follow the example of the wise virgins who, not knowing when the bridegroom might come, kept a supply of oil on hand for their lamps. (Matthew 25:1-13). He calls us to live as faithful and wise servants who will be found feeding others when their master returns to his household. (Matthew 24:45-51)

This has not been a book about the end times. Rather, it has attempted only to chronicle and comment on a spiritual revival among the Jewish people. According to the Bible, however, the restoration of Israel signals, or at minimum relates to, the end of the age. So if we wish to be like the sons and daughters of Issachar, the wise virgins or the faithful servants, we must seek the Lord to understand and know what we—and Israel—should do.

First of all, to understand the times, we must understand that God has not forsaken His people whom He foreknew. Israel has stumbled but not beyond recovery. Because of their sin, salvation has come to the Gentiles, in order to make Israel jealous. Since Israel's sin has resulted in riches for the Gentiles, their restoration will bring even greater blessing to the world. It will mean life from the dead.

Peter described a foretaste of that day when he preached to the Jews in Jerusalem. The apostle connected Israel's repentance with times of refreshing and God sending the Messiah. "Repent," he told them, "and turn to God, so that times of refreshing may come from the Lord, and that He may send the Christ who has been appointed for you—even Jesus." (Acts 3:19-20)

We are still probably some time away from the glorious day of Christ's return. The Bible seems to indicate certain crucial events must first transpire. According to some theologians, these are events in which Russia plays a key role.[135] In between Ezekiel's vision of Israel's revived dry bones in Chapter 37 and the return of God's glory to her in Chapter 40, is a war. Chapters 38 and 39 describe an apocalyptic invasion of the reestablished State of Israel by an alliance of armies from the north.

Ezekiel's interim prophecy is aimed against "Gog of the land of Magog, the chief prince of Meshech and Tubal." (Ezekiel 38:2) Some Bible scholars, including C. I. Scofield, have identified these as powers in the north of Euro-Asia Minor, headed by Russia.[136]

Extrabiblical writings equate Magog with the Ancient Scythians of the north who lived in the region of present-day Russia, Ukraine and other former Soviet republics. Secular history books confirm that the Scythians were among the earliest inhabitants of Russia.[137] Meshech and Tubal can be traced, respectively, to Moscow and the city of Tobolsk in Siberia.[138] Gog, it is generally believed, refers to a title and not a proper name. It is clear, however, that Gog comes from "the far north."[139] (Ezekiel 38:15; 39:2)

God Himself will summon these northern armies (Ezekiel 38:4, 16-17; 39:2) at a time when Israel is dwelling in safety. (Ezekiel 38:8) Then He will pour out His wrath and mercy on this imperious coalition. (Ezekiel 38:19-22; 39:3-6) His purpose will be to show Himself great and holy in the sight of the nations. (Ezekiel 38:16, 23; 39: 6-7, 21) The cataclysmic defeat of Gog and his horde will be so far-spread that it will take many months to bury their bodies and cleanse the land. As a result, God declares, "From that day forward, the house of Israel will know that I am the Lord their God." (Ezekiel 39:22)

Although some interpretations differ, the northern invasion probably occurs well before the Battle of Armageddon. Consequently, it would not usher in the Lord's return or the millennium. Instead, this incursion likely takes place before or during the seven-year Tribulation, during a time of ostensible peace in Israel.[140]

Socio-economic and political conditions in the former Soviet Union, especially Russia, are anything but stable. In Belarus and Ukraine, as well as the Russian Federation, Communism is already making a comeback. For this reason, we are pressed to sow and reap "while it is still day." Night is coming. For the same reason, it is not hard to imagine a scenario in which Russia spearheaded an attack à la Ezekiel's vision.

Two Messianic Jewish festivals were scheduled for the summer of 1996. One, held in Kishinev, capital city of the Republic of Moldova, was highly successful. But the festival planned for Kharkov, Ukraine, met with an opposite fate. Just days before its scheduled opening, city and regional officials banned the event. Inspired by the Orthodox Jewish community, the local Communist-oriented Religious Affairs Department flatly announced it was opposed to Messianic Judaism. For that reason alone it would not let the festival go on.

Ministry leaders were threatened with arrest and deportation, then actually fined several thousand dollars to pay for the cost of police actions taken against them. A press conference concerning the festival's cancellation was interrupted by armed police, who arrested the team's security guards. A few days later, police invaded a Shabbat service, held in a private hall the team had rented. The next day, Sunday, police and internal security forces disrupted worship services at the church which had officially sponsored the outreach. They threatened to arrest the Ukrainian pastor, as well as any Americans who would speak or sing at the service.

Eventually, the American Embassy got involved but to little avail. Messianic Jews, it was explained, have not been the only culprit. In the past couple of years, a number of other evangelical works have been brought to a halt in Ukraine, as well as other ex-Soviet republics.

Despite everything, there was still much one-on-one street evangelism in Kharkov. In addition, the team ministered informally in local churches, imparting God's heart and vision for Jewish evangelism and aliyah. At least two of these churches subsequently initiated their own ministries to Ukrainian Jews. With their help, a Messianic congregation was formed in Kharkov under indigenous leadership. Indeed, much fruit has been borne in this unlikely city. Nevertheless, how far gone is the day?

Russia remains a torn nation, without consistent direction.[141] President Yeltsin's chronic health problems have interfered substantially with his ability to navigate a course of economic growth or correction.[142] Alexander Lebed, his former strong-handed national security advisor, still vows to be the next president. Lebed threatens to lead a political reversal to old-style authoritarianism.[143] He actively promoted the restriction of religious freedom, declaring that only Russian Orthodoxy, Islam and Buddhism had a right to be practiced in Russia.[144]

Under a flailing Yeltsin administration, Communist and ultra-nationalist factions conspire quietly against democratic reform. According to a key Zhirinovsky aide, "The (ultra-nationalist) goal now is to grow like a cancer, to build our party at the grassroots and make Zhirinovsky more acceptable to the mainstream. Then, in five or ten years, he could burst through."[145]

The Russian Federation is not unlike a volcano that could erupt at any time, spewing its firestorm throughout the former Soviet region. Neither the Zyuganov-led Communists nor the ultra-nationalists under Zhirinovsky make secret their plans to resurrect an imperialist

Russian confederacy. They would restore authority to the Russian Orthodox Church to regulate all religious activities and eliminate evangelism from the West. In their ideal society, Jews would have no place at all,[146] for it was the Jews, they still say, that caused the collapse of the Soviet Union.[147]

A 250-page report by the Union of Councils for Soviet Jews,[148] *Anti-Semitism in the Former Soviet Union, 1995-1997*, presents statistics indicating anti-Semitism and human rights abuses are widespread in Russia and other CIS republics. The report states that anti-Semitism is so pervasive and persistent in Russia that it is considered "normal," even by Jews. Hate crimes against Russian Jews have increased but are rarely prosecuted. The spread of free speech has resulted in the widespread production and distribution of anti-Semitic publications, not only by private groups, but by local government agencies and the Russian Orthodox Church. Anti-Semitism has become the rhetoric of nationalists, Communists and fascists who oppose democratic reform.

Apart from its enduring anti-Jewish undercurrent, Russia has also taken serious steps to restrict foreign missionary activity. By 1996, an atmosphere of religious intolerance had resulted from the combined forces of nationalism, foreign cult missionary activity and the antipathy of the Russian Orthodox Church.[149] Numerous regional and city governments had, by then, enacted laws limiting evangelism.[150] In September 1997, the Russian Orthodox Church finally forced through the Parliament its new, highly restrictive religion law. Many months of protests and threats from the United States, the international human rights community, the church worldwide, and even the Vatican, did not prevent the law's passage.[151]

Under the new law, the Russian Orthodox Church is enshrined as the country's preeminent religion and an "inalienable part" of Russian history. Other traditional faiths, including Islam, Buddhism, some forms of Christianity and Judaism are to be "respected" and state-registered. However, religious groups must have had at least three congregations registered officially for 15 years (i.e., during the Soviet era) to obtain national standing. Since a few Baptist and Pentecostal groups did exist during that time, congregations registered under those denominations can remain.

Other evangelical churches, including Messianic congregations, may be forced to go underground. The law technically requires that they register with local authorities and be strictly monitored for 15 years. During that time, they will be prohibited from formally evangelizing, developing educational programs, publishing or distributing religious literature, or inviting foreign missionaries or preachers into the country.[152] Already, cases of arbitrary and capricious enforcement of the law to shut down born again churches have been documented.[153]

The minister of Moscow's Evangelical Christian Church summarized the feelings of Russia's evangelical community over the new law: "With this law signed, you can't really speak about Russia as a democratic country . . . The law is aimed at stifling all dissent. It establishes the Orthodox Church . . . in the same position the Communist Party held in the past."[153]

Despite the air of gloom, the leadership of the Messianic Center in St. Petersburg was determined to stay optimistic. "We knew such a thing could happen. We are used to many crazy laws here. Somehow we will survive," said one of the Russian ministry workers. I remembered how these new believers had shined during our second mission to Moscow-St. Petersburg two years earlier. We knew then that God was preparing them for what lay ahead. The gates of hell would not prevail against them.

Russia is not alone in its attempted backlash against the work of the Holy Spirit. Other former Soviet republics, including Ukraine and Belarus, have significantly tightened restrictions on missionary work. In Belarus, as well as Uzbekistan, Kazakhstan and Kyrgzstan, evangelistic activity is now technically limited to church buildings— and very few evangelical churches own their own buildings.[154]

Belarus has increasingly resorted to Soviet-style repressive tactics in the realm of human rights.[155] By 1997, foreign journalists were arrested and threatened for disagreeing with government policies,[156] peaceable protesters were beaten by the militia, and the President was scrapping much of the country's post-Soviet constitution.[157] Reportedly, anti-Semitism was growing more rapidly in Belarus than in other former Soviet republics.[158] Further economic decline and dictatorship-style government in Belarus could have a destabilizing ripple effect across the entire region.[159] In particular, Belarus' formal political reunion with Russia could prove dangerous for democracy for both countries.[160]

Relations between Russia and Israel have become increasingly strained. For a period of several months in 1996-7, Russia forcibly shut down aliyah operations by the Jewish Agency, Israel's emigration assistance bureau.[161] The closure of several Agency offices was ostensibly based on bureaucratic technicalities. Nonetheless, it worried Jews around the world, as Russia openly resents Israel's active promotion of aliyah.[162] The curb on aliyah came amid a presidential campaign that also unleashed a fresh flow of anti-Semitic propaganda.[163]

The Russian Federation continues to stand against Israel's aggressive efforts to eradicate terrorism and is actively building a nuclear reactor in Iran.[164] Russia has made known that it wants to play a much bigger role in Mideast politics.[165] Her sympathetic response to Iraq during the 1998 Persian Gulf Crisis belies one of her primary interests: oil.

Israel, in the meantime, is at odds with its own people and destiny. God makes it clear that the land of Israel belongs to Him, and the Jews have been entrusted with its custodial care.[166] Leviticus 25:23 says, "the land must not be sold permanently because this land is Mine and you are but aliens and My tenants." To the nations that would try to slice up the land, He warns, "I will gather all nations and bring them down to the valley of Jehoshaphat. There I will enter into judgment against them...for they scattered My people among the nations and divided up My land." (Joel 3:2; Ezekiel 36:5) Nonetheless, under the Oslo Accords, Israel has been forced to trade land for the elusive promise of peace with its Arab neighbors. All the while, radical insurgent Muslim forces are still at holy war. They will stop, they say, at nothing short of Israel's destruction.

Growing numbers of Israelis, including immigrants from the former Soviet Union,[167] are opposed to the peace-at-any-price process. Terrorist strikes within the Jewish State have not abated. Civil discord, tragically reflected in the assassination of former Prime Minister Rabin, is high in the battle-weary Jewish State.

Jewish believers in Israel, who numbered approximately 5,000 in

1997, have yet another serious concern. Political gains attained by Orthodox Jewish parties have made them an essential and influential part of Netanyahu's coalition government.[168] Now they are attempting with greater fervor than ever to abrogate the rights of Messianic Jews to make aliyah, alleging these believers are no longer Jews. Messianic citizens are also being increasingly threatened with confiscation of their identity papers and passports.[169]

Recent steps taken to restrict evangelistic activities[170] have culminated in the Israeli Parliament's giving preliminary approval to a new anti-missionary bill. The law would quite severely curtail any Messianic ministry in the land. The printing, distribution or possession of evangelical materials would be a crime punishable by imprisonment.[171] The mere proposal of the law has affected the general attitude toward believers in Israel. Anti-missionaries have increased their campaigns and activities.[172] As of this writing, believers in the land have called upon Christians and human rights proponents around the world to stand with them in protest of the bill.[173]

❖ ❖ ❖ ❖

"The watchman says, 'Morning comes but also night. If you would inquire, inquire....'" (Isaiah 21:12, NAS) Like the people of Issachar, we inquire: What are we to do?

Foremost, we are to pray. Psalm 122:6 says, "Pray for the peace of Jerusalem: 'May they prosper who love you.'" (NAS) God is calling the church to intercede for the peace of Jerusalem and all of Israel.[174] Perhaps the current peace accord is, despite its problems, divinely inspired. If it is, a resulting period of temporary peace might prove to be only the biblical prelude to a northern invasion. But a lull in hostilities could also signal a quiet season with unprecedented opportunities for evangelism in the Mideast. On the other hand, significant disruption with the peace process could mean imminent war for Israel and large-scale terrorism.

One thing is sure: there will be no lasting peace in Israel apart from the rule and reign of the Prince of Peace. *Pray for the church in Israel, especially her Messianic Jews.*[175] *Pray also for the salvation of the unbelieving Jewish people in the Land, in your community, and worldwide.* Ask God to give you the Father's heart for this prodigal people. As He reveals does, experience the surprising delights of the depths of His mercy.

Intercede especially for the Jewish people upon whom the Holy Spirit is so profoundly moving, those in the former Soviet Union. Ask the Lord of the harvest to send laborers into these ripe fields. Pray for those whom He has already sent; Jewish evangelists face fierce opposition. Even the apostle Paul needed the Gentile church to stand in the gap for him on account of his unbelieving Jewish brethren. (Romans 15:31) According to Scripture, the Messianic remnant of Israel is bitterly hated by the enemy and targeted for opposition: "Then the dragon was enraged at the woman [i.e., Israel] and went off to make war against the rest of her offspring, those who obey God's commandments *and hold to the testimony of Jesus.*" (Revelation 12:17, emphasis added) Those who hold to the testimony of Jesus are Messianic Jews.

Now is God's time for the Jews of the Land of the North to go home to Israel. Pray that multitudes will return as born again believers, like unquenchable firebrands. Up to a quarter of Israel's Messianic Jews are recent immigrants from the former Soviet Union. Russian Jewish immigrants have already formed a political party that is impacting the nation in positive ways.[176]

Pray for God to move on the hearts of Jews worldwide to make aliyah. Lift up to the throne of grace the Israeli government's persistent refusal to let Messianic Jews make aliyah. Thankfully, ex-Soviet Jewish believers have been able to slip into the country without difficulty. The situation has been different for those living in the West. In North America alone, hundreds, if not thousands, of Messianic Jews would likely move to Israel if legally allowed to enter.[177] Remember that, if genocidal anti-Semitism sweeps the globe, these brothers and sisters in the faith will have nowhere to go if Israel's doors remain shut to them.

As you pray for the peace of Jerusalem, be willing to be a vehicle for the answer to your prayers. Ask for Spirit-led opportunities to sincerely befriend and truthfully share the gospel with unsaved Jews. God has anointed the church to "provoke to jealousy" the Jewish people. (Romans 11:14, KJV) Indeed, the church has often provoked them— but not to jealousy. Instead of condemnation, bring comfort: "'Comfort, comfort My people,' says your God. 'Speak tenderly to Jerusalem and proclaim to her that her hard service has been completed, that her sin has been paid for....'" (Isaiah 40:1-2) Tell your Jewish friend, as the Spirit leads, that in Messiah, her sin has been paid for. As you do, sincerely love your friend with Messiah's love.

Remain sensitive to your friend's need to retain his or her Jewish identity. Use language and concepts that reflect the Jewish character of the New Testament (e.g., "Messiah" rather than "Christ"). If you feel you need more information or help on witnessing to Jews, any Messianic congregation or Jewish evangelistic ministry (including Hear O Israel Ministries) should gladly give it to you.

Pray for the former Soviet bloc countries and their leaders. Many millions of people in these lands are spiritually hungry and have not yet heard the gospel message. As more and more of them come to faith, they are faced with a serious shortage of properly trained indigenous leaders.[178] Pray about personally participating in, or financially supporting, short- or long-term missionary work. We do not know how long the doors will stay open there for the preaching of the gospel. When the doors eventually shut to outsiders, pray the underground church in the CIS will be strong in the Lord. Pray, too, concerning the northern armies' future invasion of Israel, that in wrath God would remember mercy (Habakkuk 3:2), for the sake of the Russians as well as the Jews.

In addition to prayer, identify as a Christian with your Old Testament Jewish heritage. As we have already seen, the Bible teaches that believing Gentiles have been grafted like wild branches into a Jewish olive tree:

". . .If the root is holy, so are the branches. But if some of the branches have been broken off, and you, though a wild olive shoot, have been grafted in among the others and now share in the nourishing sap from the olive root, do not boast over those branches. If you do, consider this: You do not support the root, but the root supports you. You will say then, 'Branches were broken off so that I could be grafted in.' Granted. But they were broken off because of unbelief, and you stand by faith. Do not be arrogant but be afraid. For if God did not spare the natural branches, He will not spare you, either . . . And if they do not persist in unbelief, they will be grafted in, for God is able to graft them in again. After all, if you were cut out of an olive tree that is wild by nature and, contrary to nature, were grafted into a cultivated olive tree, how much more readily will these, the natural branches, be grafted into their own olive tree!" (Romans 11:16-21, 23-24)

When Paul penned this metaphor, it was the practice in Israel to invigorate an olive tree that had ceased to bear fruit by grafting it with a shoot of a wild olive. The sap, or life-blood, of the wild olive branches would revive the cultivated tree. Then the original branches would begin again to bear fruit. Similarly, the wild branches would produce such good and plentiful fruit as would otherwise never be possible.[179] When Gentiles who have been grafted into a Jewish-rooted faith function as God intended, great fruit results!

It is possible for the church to affiliate with its Old Testament heritage without trying to replace the natural branches. The grafting agents are humility, love and dedication to biblical truth. Many Gentile believers have found God richly reveals Himself as they incorporate biblically Jewish elements or, as Jesus called them, "old treasures" (Matthew 13:52), into their lives. The feasts of Israel, for example, all point to Christ, Whose Spirit fills them with fresh meaning.

Bear in mind that the church's future is replete with Hebraic worship. Ezekiel's vision of a new temple includes sacrificial offerings. (Ezekiel 40-48) During Christ's rule on earth, all nations will participate annually in the Feast of Tabernacles in Jerusalem. (Zechariah 14:16) They will come regularly to the house of the God of Jacob to be taught from the law. (Isaiah 2:3) Sabbaths and new moons will be observed. (Isaiah 66:23) As you embrace your Jewish roots, you will naturally come to love and identify with your Messianic brethren, with whom you form one new man.

If you wish to support Israel in a tangible way, remember your Jewish brothers and sisters in the faith. Investigate the extent to which any organization or ministry you may wish to support is willing, in turn, to actually support Jews who place their trust in Christ.

The Bible teaches that Israel's salvation is connected to the return of the Lord. The disciples once asked Jesus what the sign would be of His coming and the end of the age. One sign, He replied, would be the fulfillment of the times of the Gentiles. This would occur when Jerusalem was no longer trodden down by the Gentiles. (Luke 21:7-28) Gentile control over Jerusalem began to lift when the Jews recaptured the city in 1967. Another sign, Jesus said, would be Jerusalem's cry, "Blessed is he who comes in the name of the Lord." (Matthew 23:39) This is now the prayer of multitudes of Jews in the Land of the North—and a growing minority in Jerusalem itself. These signs, together with others, would seem to indicate the beginning of the end is upon us.

Paul explained that a hardening in part has come upon Israel until the fullness of the Gentiles comes in. But then, he said, all Israel[180] would be saved. (Romans 11:25-26) The prophet Zechariah foresaw that glorious day:

"I am going to make Jerusalem a cup that sends all the surrounding peoples reeling. Judah will be besieged as well as Jerusalem. On that day, when all the nations of the earth are gathered against her, I will make Jerusalem an immovable rock for all the nations ... On that day, I will set out to destroy all the nations that attack Jerusalem. And I will pour out on the house of David and the inhabitants of Jerusalem a spirit of grace and supplication. They will look on Me, the one they have pierced, and they will mourn for Him as one mourns for an only child, and grieve bitterly for Him as one grieves for a first-born son ... Then the Lord will go out and fight against those nations, as He fights in the day of battle. On that day, His feet will stand on the Mount of Olives, east of Jerusalem ... On that day, living water will flow out from Jerusalem, half to the eastern sea and half to the western sea, in summer and in winter. The Lord will be king over the whole earth. On that day, there will be one Lord, and His name is the only name." (Zechariah 12:2-3, 9-10; 14:3-4, 8-9)

According to both the Old and New Testaments, Israel's repentance ushers in Yeshua's return. So, to pray for her salvation is, in effect, to pray for the salvation of the nations, for life from the dead, for the return of the King!

Finally, prepare your heart to meet the Lord. It is important to remember that Messiah's return, though glorious, involves divine judgment and tribulation of unprecedented proportions. It is incumbent upon every believer to prepare his or her heart in holiness. Loving God's covenant people Israel will assuredly help you do just that.

✧ ✧ ✧ ✧

Some of you who have read this book may have never given your life to Yeshua. In these pages, you have read about what the Bible says concerning Israel's Messiah. He is the Lord of love. Despite how He has been misrepresented by man for over 2,000 years, the Bible says: ". . .God so loved the world that He gave His only begotten Son, that whoever believes in Him should not perish but have eternal life. For God did not send the Son into the world to judge the world but that the world should be saved through Him." (John 3:16-17, NAS)

According to Isaiah 64:6: "All of us have become like one who is unclean, and all our righteous acts are like filthy rags." As a result, the prophet says, "Your iniquities have separated you from your God; your sins have hidden His face from you, so that He will not hear." (Isaiah 59:2) Nonetheless, because of God's love, there is good news: "All have sinned and fall short of the glory of God, and are justified freely by His grace through the redemption that came through Christ Jesus." (Romans 3:23-24)

The Old Testament law provided for the forgiveness of sin through the sacrificially shed blood of an innocent animal. Under the New Covenant (Jeremiah 31:31-34), the sacrificially shed blood of the Lamb of God, our sinless Messiah, cleanses us from all sin. (Hebrews 9:12-10:18) "If you confess with your mouth, 'Jesus (Yeshua) is Lord,' and believe in your heart that God raised Him from the dead, you will be saved." (Romans 10:9)

Whether you are Jewish or Gentile, you can receive God's gift of eternal life through Yeshua, right now, wherever you are. All your sins will be forgiven and you will be a new person. The Bible says, "Therefore, if anyone is in Christ, he is a new creation; the old has gone, the new has come." (II Corinthians 5:17) All you need to do is confess to the Creator of the Universe that you have fallen short of His glory, broken His law, and sinned. Ask Him to forgive you through Yeshua's sacrificial atonement. Believe in faith that Messiah bore your personal sins on the cross 2,000 years ago. Commit your life to Him. Ask Him to come into your heart by His Holy Spirit. Believe He has heard you and delights to do what you have just asked. Then, thank Him and rejoice!

If you have just given your life to Yeshua, you now have a personal relationship with the one true God and the Messiah of Israel! Your name is written in His Book of Life! If you do not have a Bible, please obtain one as soon as possible. Read it every day. Pray often. Last but by no means least, please contact a Bible-believing church or Messianic congregation in your community. Let them know of your new-found faith so they can help you grow in it.

If you have not given your life to the Lord but are a sincere seeker of truth, God will still respond to you. Simply ask Him to show you if what the Bible teaches is true. Ask Him to show you, in however long or short a time it may take, if Jesus is, in fact, the Messiah—but be genuinely wanting and willing to get an answer! If you have a Bible, you may wish to read Old Testament prophecies predicting who the Messiah will be.[181] Ask the Lord to speak to you as you read His Word. Trust that He will!

"Now to Him who is able to establish you by [the] gospel and the proclamation of Jesus Christ, according to the revelation of the mystery hidden for long ages past, but now revealed and made know through the prophetic writings by the command of the eternal God, so that all nations might believe and obey Him, to the only wise God be glory forever through Jesus Christ! Amen."   Romans 16:25-27

Endnotes

[1]   Consistent with its biblical usage, the term "Israel" refers here not only to the land of Israel but to the people of Israel, i.e., the Jews, whether or not they happen to live in the land.

[2]   Medron Medzini, "From the Last Reservoirs," *The Jerusalem Post, International Edition:* p. 22, March 29, 1997.

[3]   See, for example, Psalms 102:12-16, Isaiah 52: 7-10, Zechariah 12:10-14:9, Matthew 23:39 and Romans 11:11-15, 25-27.

[4]   In the words of high profile American rabbi Daniel Lapin, "For most American Jews, the only belief they hold in common is that Jesus was not the Messiah. That's the one thing that defines you as a Jew. I think that's pathetic. You can't define a religious identity by what you don't believe. . ." Bob Jones, "Deuteronomy Duo," *World* (February 15, 1997): 15.

[5]   For a thorough discussion on the subject of anti-Semitism in the Christian church, see Michael L. Brown, *Our Hands Are Stained with Blood* (Shippensburg, PA; Destiny Image Publishers, 1992); and Hal Lindsay, *The Road to Holocaust* (New York: Bantam Books, 1989). For additional material, see Fr. Edward H. Flannery, *The Anguish of the Jews: Twenty-Three Centuries of Anti-Semitism* (New York: Paulist Press, 1985), pp. 47-160; David A. Rausch, *A Legacy of Hatred: Why Christians Must Not Forget the Holocaust* (Chicago, IL: Moody Press, 1984), pp. 16-30, 163-206; Max I. Dimont, *The Indestructible Jews* (New York: Signet, 1973), pp. 270-291, 370-385; John G. Gager, *The Origins of Anti-Semitism: Attitudes Toward Judaism in Pagan and Christian Antiquity* (New York: Oxford University Press, 1983), pp. 117-173, 197-229; Jakob Jocz, *The*

Jewish People and Jesus Christ, 3d ed. (Grand Rapids, MI: Baker Book House, 1979), pp. 76-98; and, generally, *The Origins of the Holocaust: Christian Anti-Semitism*, Randolph L. Branham, ed., (New York: Columbia University Press, 1986); Fred G. Bratton, *The Crime of Christendom: The Theological Sources of Christian Anti-Semitism* (Boston, MA: Beacon Press, 1969); Jacques Doukhan, *Drinking at the Sources*, Walter R. Beach and Robert M. Johnston, transl. (Mountain View, CA: Pacific Press Publishing Assoc., 1981).

[6] As recently as July, 1997, a mass grave of victims of Stalin's 1937-38 purges was discovered and unearthed in a pine forest north of St. Petersburg. The discovery of the remains of at least 1,111 prisoners came after a search which lasted nearly a decade. David Hoffman, "Site of 1,100 Stalinist Executions Found," *The Washington Post* (July 13, 1997): p. A21.

[7] Estimates of the numbers of Jews in the CIS are extremely difficult to ascertain and vary widely. Because anti-Semitism is so prevalent, many are unwilling to identify themselves as Jews to census takers. Others do not know for sure if they are Jewish because past generations similarly denied their heritage for fear of persecution. In addition there is much ambiguity surrounding the definition of who is a Jew. See, for example, Robert J. Brym, *The Jews of Moscow, Kiev and Minsk: Identity, Anti-Semitism and Emigration* (Washington Square, NY: New York University Press, 1994), pp. 19-21; Mary Jane Behrends Clark, *The Commonwealth of Independent States* (Brookfield, CT: The Millbrook Press, 1992), p. 25. Estimates herein are based on the 1989 official census of the Soviet Union, together with 1995 unofficial data from the National Conference on Soviet Jewry, the Hebrew Immigrant Aid Society and Hear O Israel Ministries.

[8] For a thorough discussion on anti-Semitism in Russia and the former Soviet Union see, generally, Salo W. Baron, *The Russian Jew Under Tsars and Soviets* 2nd ed. (New York: MacMillan Publishing Co., Inc., 1976); Benjamin Pinkus, *The Jews of the Soviet Union: The History of a National Minority* (Cambridge, MA: Cambridge University Press, 1988); *Anti-Semitism in the Soviet*

Union: Its Roots and Consequences, Theodore Freedman, ed., (New York: Freedom Library Press of the Anti-Defamation League of B'nai B'rith, 1984); Harry G. Shaffer, *The Soviet Treatment of Jews* (New York: Praeger Publishing, Inc., 1974); Joel Cang, *The Silent Millions: A History of the Jews in the Soviet Union* (New York: Taplinger Publishing Co., 1970); "Russia," *Encyclopedia Judaica*, vol. 14 (Jerusalem: Keter Publishing House Jerusalem, Ltd., 1972), pp. 434-505. See also John Shelton Curtiss, *Church and State in Russia* (New York: Octagon Books, 1972), pp. 339-340; Flannery, *Anguish of the Jews*, pp. 170-174, 230-246; Carrie Hart, "Jews Need Divine Help as Anti-Semitism Rises," *Charisma* (September 1995): pp. 16-17; "Anti-Semitism," *Encyclopedia Judaica*, vol. 3, pp. 123-160; "Anti-Semitic Political Parties and Organizations," *Encyclopedia Judaica*, vol. 3, p. 86.

9 Keith L. Brooks, *The Jews and the Passion for Palestine in the Light of Prophecy* (Grand Rapids, MI; Zondervan Publishing House, 1937), pp. 51-57; "Protocols of the Elders of Zion," *Encyclopedia Judaica*, vol. 6, pp. 581-583; Brym, *Jews of Moscow, Kiev and Minsk*, pp. 41-43; "United States," *Encyclopedia Judaica*, vol. 15, p. 1653; Lawrence Elliott, "This Lie Will Not Die," *Reader's Digest* (April 1995), pp. 115-119; Brown, *Hands Are Stained*, p. 66.

In 1934 an international libel suit based on the book was held in Switzerland. At the trial, the defendants (Nazis) claimed *The Protocols* were written at the First International Zionist Congress in 1897. The court determined that Russian secret agents had forged it from another work entitled "A Dialogue in Hell." The book is still influential among hate groups around the world, including some in the US.

10 Baron, *The Russian Jew*, pp. 317-321; Caroline Arnold and Herma Silverstein, *Anti-Semitism: A Modern Perspective* (New York: Julian Messner, 1985), pp. 86-90; Cang, *Silent Millions*, p. 202; Pinkus, *Jews of the Soviet Union*, pp. 245-260; William Korey, *The Soviet Cage: Anti-Semitism in Russia* (New York: The Viking Press, 1973), pp. 165-328; William Korey, "The Soviet Public Anti-Zionist Committee: An Analysis," in *Soviet Jewry in the 1980s: The Politics of Anti-Semitism and Emigration and the Dynamics of Resettlement*, ed., Robert O.

Freedman (Durham, NC: Duke University Press, 1989), pp. 26-50. For an interesting and insightful discussion on the subject, see the autobiographical account of well-known Soviet refusenik Natan Sharansky, *Fear No Evil* (New York: Random House, Inc., 1988).

[11] For an interesting account from a Christian perspective predicting an exodus of Jews from the Soviet Union, see Steve Lightle, *Exodus II: Let My People Go!* (Kingwood, TX: Hunter Books, 1983) which also relates some of the repercussions endured by Soviet Jews trying to emigrate to Israel.

[12] Mark 1:17; Luke 5:10.

[13] For a timely comment on this issue, see Carrie Hart, "Russians Attack Jew-Lover Church," *Charisma* (September 1995), p. 18.

[14] See, for example, Rausch, *Legacy of Hatred*, pp. 41-66, 162-169; Doukhan, *Drinking at the Sources*, pp. 38-39; Warren B. Morris, Jr., *The Weimer Republic and Nazi Germany* (Chicago, IL: Nelson-Hall, 1982), pp. 187-189; and, generally, David Abraham, *The Collapse of the Weimer Republic*, 2d. ed., (New York: Holmes and Meier, 1986).

[15] Mark Hitchcock, *After The Empire - Bible Prophecy in Light of the Fall of the Soviet Union* (Wheaton, IL: Tyndale House Publishers, Inc., 1994), pp. 41-54; Reuters, "Zhirinovsky Hails Buchanan, Says Could Deport Jews" (February 22, 1996); Hart, "Russians Attack," *Charisma*; Zoya Krakhmalnikova, "The Ideology of Schism," *Izvestiya* (Moscow: April 19, 1994) translated and reprinted in *RCDA* vol. 32, no. 2 (1993-94), pp. 24-26.

[16] Nicolas Zernov, *Eastern Christendom* (New York: G. P. Putnam's Sons, 1961), p. 111; John S. Curtiss, *The Russian Church and the Soviet State: 1900-1917* (NY: Octagon Books, 1972), pp. 6-7; Pinkus, *Jews of the Soviet Union*, pp. 4-5; Sergei Pushkarev, Vladimir Rusak and Gleb Yakunin, *Christianity and Government in Russia and the Soviet Union: Reflections on the Millennium* (Boulder, CO: Westview Press, Inc., 1989), pp. 35-36; "Russian Orthodox Church," *The*

Encyclopedia of Religion, vol. 12 (New York: Macmillian Publishing Co., 1987), p. 488; "Russia," *World Book Encyclopedia*, vol. 16 (World Book, Inc., 1994), p. 548.

17 Pinkus, *Jews of the Soviet Union,* pp. 4-5; Edward H. Judge, *Easter In Kishinev: Anatomy of a Pogrom* (New York: New York University Press, 1992), pp. 2-4.

18 George P. Fedotov, *The Russian Religious Mind*, vol. 1 (Cambridge, MA: Harvard University Press, 1946) pp. 74-75, 84-93, 382; Baron, *The Russian Jew*, pp. 4-5; "Eastern Orthodoxy," *Encyclopedia Brittanica*, Vol. 17, 15th ed. (Chicago, IL: Encyclopedia Brittanica, 1995), pp. 843-844; Jane Ellis, *The Russian Orthodox Church - A Contemporary History* (Bloomington, IN: Indiana University Press, 1986), p. 7; "Anti-Semitism," *Encyclopedia Judaica*, vol. 3, p. 123.

19 Ibid.

20 Freedman, *Anti-Semitism in the Soviet Union*, pp. 8-9; Judge, *Easter in Kishinev*, p. 5; Baron, *The Russian Jew*, pp. 6, 17-18; Nicholas V. Riasanovsky, *A History of Russia*, 4th ed. (New York: Oxford University Press, Inc., 1984), pp. 394-396.

21 Baron, *The Russian Jew*, pp. 32-33; Pinkus, *The Jews of the Soviet Union*, p. 13; Bratton, *Crime of Christendom*, pp. 152-153; Riasanovsky, *A History of Russia*, p. 395; "Russia," *Encyclopedia Judaica*, vol. 14, p. 436; "Pale of Jewish Settlement," *Encyclopedia Judaica*, vol. 13, pp. 24-28.

22 See, for example, Korey, *The Soviet Cage*, pp. 24-25, which refers to the passport or identity card system, with its "nationality" restriction: and, Pinkus, *The Jews of the Soviet Union*, pp. 210-216; Brym, *The Jews of Moscow, Kiev and Minsk*, p. 19.

23 See, generally, Fedotov, *The Russian Religious Mind*; "Russian Orthodox Church," *The Encyclopedia of Religion,* vol. 12, p. 488 ff.; Ellis, *The Russian Orthodox Church*, p. 7; Krakhmalnikova, "Ideology," *RCDA*, pp. 25-26; William C. Fletcher, *The Russian*

Orthodox Church Underground: 1917-1970 (London: Oxford University Press, 1971), p. 193.

[24] See, for example, Curtiss, *Church and State,* pp. 255-283, 336-340. As to the church's continued tolerance of anti-Semitism, see Michael Bordeaux, *The Gospel's Triumph Over Communism* (Minneapolis, MN: Bethany House Publishers, 1991), pp. 107, 210.

[25] Pushkarev, *Christianity and Government,* pp. 1-44; Curtiss, *Church and State,* pp. 6-86; Gerlad Buss, *The Bear's Hug: Christian Belief and the Soviet State, 1917-1986* (Grand Rapids, MI: Wm. B. Eerdmans Publishing Co., 1987), pp. 13, 172-186; Ellis, *The Russian Orthodox Church,* pp. 253-262; Ernst Benz, *The Eastern Orthodox Church,* Richard and Clara Winston, transl. (Chicago, IL: Aldine Publishing Co., 1963) pp. 211-212; Dimitri Pospielovsky, *The Russian Church Under the Soviet Regime 1917-1982,* vol. 2 (Crestwood, NY: St. Vladimir's Seminary Press, 1984), p. 469-470; Gretta Palmer, *God's Underground* (NY: Appleton-Century-Crofts, Inc., 1949) p. viii; J.N. Danzas, *The Russian Church,* Olga Bennigsen, transl. (NY: Sheed and Ward, 1936) pp. 26, 33-34, 106-107, 116-118; "Anti-Semitism," *Encyclopedia Judaica,* vol. 3, p. 123; Krakhmalnikova, "Ideology," *RCDA,* p. 26; "Russian Orthodox Church," *Encyclopedia of Religion,* vol. 12, pp. 490-491; "Eastern Orthodoxy," *Encyclopedia Brittanica,* vol. 17, pp. 843-44; Lee Hockstader, "Russian Orthodox Church Is Feeling Rebirth Pains—Critics Accuse It Of Coziness With Government," *The Washington Post* (April 15, 1996): p. A16.

[26] See, for example, Daniel B. Rowland, "Moscow—The Third Rome or the New Israel?" *The Russian Review,* vol. 55 (October 1996): p. 591.

[27] Harvey Fireside, *Icon and Swastika: The Russian Orthodox Church Under Nazi and Soviet Control* (Cambridge, MA: Harvard University Press, 1971), pp. 2, 5, 190-192; Kent R. Hill, *The Puzzle of the Soviet Church: An Inside Look at Christianity and Glasnost* (Portland, OR: Multnomah Press, 1989), pp. 101-135; Buss, *The Bear's Hug,* pp. 172-186; Benz, *Eastern Orthodox Church,* p. 211-212; Riasanovsky, *A History of Russia,* p. 588; "Russian Orthodox

Church," *Encyclopedia of Religion*, vol. 12, pp. 490-491; Ellis, *The Russian Orthodox Church*, pp. 253-262; Michael Bordeaux, *The Gospel's Triumph*, pp. 44, 87, 101, 161, 190; Palmer, *God's Underground*, p. viii.

28 Sergius Bulgakov, *The Orthodox Church* (New York: Mohawk Publishing Co., 1935), pp. 18, 48-57, 149-164; Alexander Schmemann, *The Historical Road of Eastern Orthodoxy* (New York: Holt, Rinehart & Winston, Inc., 1963), p. 319; Fedotov, *The Russian Religious Mind*, pp. 179-201; Monk Fr. Mitrofan, *Holy Russia Inside the Soviet Union* (Minneapolis, MN: Light & Life Publishing Co., 1989), p. 27; R. M. French, *The Eastern Orthodox Church* (London: Hutchinson University Library, 1951), pp. 118-119; Hockstader, "Russian Orthodox Church," *The Washington Post*, p. A16; Daniel B. Clendenin, "Why I'm Not Orthodox," *Christianity Today* (January 6, 1997): pp. 34-37; *The Voice of the Martyrs*, (July 1995), p. 3.

After completing my research for this book on the Russian Orthodox Church, its doctrine and liturgy, I attended a worship service during a subsequent mission in the CIS. I found it very much as the above sources had described. As we left, my translator and I stopped to look at an enormous painting that hung on the wall of the sanctuary. It depicted Mary lying in a coffin, a man bowing before her body. The man's oversized hands were cut off at the wrists and hung in mid-air over his head. My young translator discreetly asked one of the parishioners what this icon was about. The middle-aged woman astonished us both with her ire. "Shame on you for not knowing this!" she scolded. "You should know—it is in the Bible—that man tried to touch the Blessed Virgin, so the angel had to cut off his hands!" Quite a lesson indeed.

29 Beverly Nickles, "Will Growing Nationalism Stall Christian Outreach," *Christianity Today* (August 12, 1996), p. 54.

30 For discussion on the persecuted church in the former Soviet Union, see, generally, Very Rev. D. Konstantinow, *Stations of the Cross: The Russian Orthodox Church 1970-1980*, S. I. Lee, transl. (London: Zaria Publishing Co., 1984); Bishop Richard J. Cooke, *Religion in Russia Under the Soviets* (New York: The Abingdon

Press, 1942); Fletcher, *Church Underground*; Fireside, *Icon and Swastika*; Hill, *Puzzle of the Soviet Church*; Palmer, *God's Underground*; Buss, *The Bear's Hug*, pp. 76-154, 172-186; James and Marti Hefley, *By Their Blood: Christian Martyrs of the Twentieth Century* (Grand Rapids, MI: Baker Book House, 1988), pp. 225-258; Bordeaux, *The Gospel's Triumph*, pp. 1-13.

[31] According to Alexander Yakovlev, President of the Russian Commission for the Rehabilitation of Victims of Political Oppression, during the years of Communism, 200,000 clergymen alone were killed from 1917-1985. Many of these were tortured brutally. *Voice of the Martyrs* (April 1996), p. 4, citing *Idea* (December 7, 1995). See also, Riasanovsky, *A History of Russia*, p. 588.

[32] Thomas S. McCall and Zola Levitt, *Coming: The End! Russia and Israel in Prophecy* (Chicago, IL: Moody Press, 1992), pp. 77-78; Dan N. Jacobs, "Afterword: Is There a Future for Jews in the USSR?" in *We Are Leaving Mother Russia: Chapters in The Russian Jewish Experience*, Scott M. Olitzky, ed. (Cincinnati, OH: The American Jewish Archives), pp. 69-70; Bordeaux, *The Gospel's Triumph*, p. 210; Howard Spier, "Soviet Anti-Semitism Unchained: The Rise of the Historical and Patriotic Association, Pamyat," in Freedman, *Soviet Jewry*, pp. 51-57; Elliott, "This Lie," *Reader's Digest* (April 1995): p. 119; V. Cherkesov, "Seeds of National Socialism in the USSR?" *Current Digest of the Soviet Press*, vol. 42, no. 9 (April 4, 1990); "Politics," *Current Digest of the Soviet Press* (November 11, 1992), pp. 25-26; Alexander Nezhny, "Has the Bride of the Lamb Joined 'Pamyat'?" *RCDA*, vol. 31, no. 3 (November 1992); Leonid Kelbert, "The Protocols of Pamyat," *Hadassah Magazine* (February 1991), p. 17; Vladimir Reznichenko, "Anti-Semitism on Trial," *Soviet Life* (February 1991), pp. 14-17; David E. Powell, "The Revival of Religion," *Current History*, vol. 90, no. 558 (October 1991), p. 330; Wendy Sloane, "Cossacks, Communists Unite in Call to Bring Back Russia's Czar," *Christian Science Monitor* (October 11, 1994), p. 7.

[33] For discussion relating to replacement theology (also sometimes called "fulfillment" or "transfer" doctrine), see Brown, *Hands Are*

Stained, pp. 117-153; Lindsey, *Holocaust*, pp. 8-11; Derek Prince, *Prophetic Destinies* (Lake Mary, FL: Creation House, 1992), pp. 13-28; John F. Walvoord, *Major Bible Prophecies* (Grand Rapids, MI: Zondervan Publishing House, 1991), pp. 59-72; John F. Walvoord, *Israel in Prophecy* (Grand Rapids, MI: Zondervan Publishing House, 1962), pp. 46-62; Arnold G. Fruchtenbaum, *Israelology: The Missing Link in Systematic Theology* (Tustin, CA: Ariel Ministries Press, 1993), pp. 43-58, 177-189.

34 "Christian Identity" theology provides an extreme but timely example of the fruits of replacement doctrine in the United States. The theology is espoused by different Christian sects, including the "Freemen" who gained notoriety as the result of their prolonged standoff with the Federal Bureau of Investigation in the spring of 1996. Christian Identity adherents claim they are the lost ten tribes of Israel, and that the Jews are descended from Satan. Laurie Goodstein, "Freemen's Theological Agenda," *The Washington Post* (April 9, 1996): p. A3.

35 An inexhaustive list of Scriptures either explicitly or implicity affirming the Abrahamic convenant includes: Genesis 13:14-17, 15:17-21, 17:18-21 (affirming the promise of the land to the descendants of Isaac, not Ishmael), 21:12, 22:15-18, 26:2-5, 26:24, 28:12-15; Leviticus 26:44-45; II Samuel 7:12-16 (Davidic covenant); Psalms 105:8-11; Jeremiah 31:31-37 (New Covenant); 33:23-26, Romans 3:1-2, 3:29, 9-11; Galatians 6:16 and Ephesians 3:6. For a thorough discussion on God's unconditional covenants with Israel, see Fruchtenbaum, *Israelology*, pp. 334-373, 570-587, 628-634.

36 Arthur W. Kac, *The Rebirth of the State of Israel: Is It of God or of Men?* (Chicago, IL: Moody Press, 1958), pp. 307-308.

37 See, for example, Lindsey, *The Road to Holocaust*, pp. 9, 57-58.

38 For discussion on hermeneutics, see, generally, Roy B. Zuck, *Basic Bible Interpretation* (Wheaton, IL: Victor Books, 1991); Bernard Ramm, *Protestant Biblical Interpretation*, 3d rev. ed. (Grand Rapids,

MI: Baker Book House, 1970); Gordon D. Fee and Douglas Stuart, *How to Read the Bible for All Its Worth* (Grand Rapids, MI: Zondervan Publishing House, 1982); Walter C. Kaiser, Jr., and Moises Silva, *An Introduction to Biblical Hermeneutics: The Search for Meaning* (Grand Rapids, MI: Zondervan Publishing House, 1994), pp. 19-45, 218-220. For discussion of the foundational role of biblical hermeneutics to understanding Israel's place in the plan of God, see Walvoord, *Israel in Prophecy*, pp. 27-46; Brown, *Hands Are Stained*, pp. 117-153; Lindsey, *Holocaust*, pp. 7-9, 53-77; Arnold G. Fruchtenbaum, *Hebrew Christianity: Its Theology, History and Philosophy* (Washington, DC: Canon Press, 1974), pp. 17-34.

[39] Zuck, *Basic Bible Interpretation*, p. 38.

[40] Lindsey, *The Road to Holocaust*, pp. 9-13; Zola Levitt, "Broken Branches: Has the Church Replaced Israel?" (Dallas, TX: ZOLA, undated pamphlet), pp. 10, 35-36.

[41] See, for example, Thomas F. Torrance, *Divine Meaning: Studies in Patristic Hermeneutics* (Edinburgh, Scotland: T & T Clark Ltd., 1995) pp. 168-170, 177-178; Kaiser and Silva, *Biblical Hermeneutics*, pp. 218-220; Zuck, *Bible Interpretation*, pp. 33-37; Fedotov, *Russian Religious Mind*, p. 384.

[42] For an insightful analysis on the meaning of "spiritual Jew," see Fruchtenbaum, *Israelology*, pp. 699-711. See also Prince, *Prophetic Destinies*, pp. 13-28, regarding Paul's use of the words "Jew" and "Israel."

[43] Paul's declaration of Israel's "advantage" must be understood in connection with his statement that "God does not show favoritism." (Romans 2:11; see also Acts 10:34-35.) Israel's advantage refers to privilege with corresponding responsibility for the good of others, namely, their entrustment with the words of God, in service to all nations. Thus, Israel's position as a chosen people leaves them on equal ground with the Gentiles with respect to salvation through faith.

44 This Scripture does not advocate either the continuation or abolition of slavery. It merely assumes its existence in the culture of that time. In fact, slavery is presumed wherever it is mentioned in the Bible. Galatians 3:28 must be read in light of that presupposition. To demonstrate the verse's continued relevance in Western culture, however, the sphere of work is considered.

45 For additional discussion on Galatians 3:28, see Fruchtenbaum, *Israelology*, pp. 712-714; *Beacon Bible Commentary,* vol. IX (Kansas City, MO: Beacon Hill Press, 1965), p. 68; Ronald Y. K. Fung, *The Epistle to the Galatians* in *The New International Commentary on the New Testament*, F. F. Bruce, ed. (Grand Rapids, MI: Wm. B. Eerdmans Publishing Co., 1988), pp. 175-176; Comment on Galatians 3:28, in Matthew Henry, *An Exposition of the Old and New Testaments*, vol. VI (New York: Fleming H. Revell Co., n.d.), n. p.; Adam Clarke, *Clarke's Commentary*, vol. V (Nashville, TN: Abingdon Press, 1977), p. 402.

46 Brown, *Hands Are Stained*, pp. 7-17, 59-67, 77-81, 89-97; Lindsey, *Holocaust*, pp. 2-78; Rausch, *Legacy of Hatred*, pp. 16-30, 163-206; Jocz, *The Jewish People*, pp. 76-98; Krakhmalnikova, "Ideology," *RCDA*, p. 26; "Anti-Semitism," *Encyclopedia Judaica*, vol. 3, pp. 99-100; Doukhan, *Drinking at the Sources*, pp. 34-39.

47 "The End of Werewolf," *Russian News* (July 7, 1994).

48 Following the destruction of the Temple and resulting interruption of the ceremonial law, the rabbis who rejected Jesus as Messiah attempted to extract and systematize their interpretation of Judaism. The resulting work, expounded upon, and eventually known as the Talmud, is a voluminous and complex maze of traditions and humanistic reasoning. See, for example, Boaz Cohen, *Everyman's Talmud* (New York: E. P. Dutton & Co., Inc., 1949), pp. viii-ix, xv, xviii; Moses Mielziner, *Introduction to the Talmud* (New York: Bloch Publishing Co., 1968), pp. 3-62; Adin Steinsaltz, *The Essential Talmud*, Chaya Galai, trans. (NY: Basic Books, Inc. 1976), pp. 3-63, 272-275. As stated in Philip Birnbaum, *A Book of Jewish Concepts* (New York: Hebrew Publishing Co., 1964), p. 637,

"the Talmud concerns itself with *every* phase of human activity" (emphasis added).

49 "Kabbalah," *Encyclopedia Judaica*, vol. 10, pp. 490-493; "Hasidim," *Encyclopedia Judaica*, vol. 7, pp. 1390, 1402, 1414-16; "Habad," *Encyclopedia Judaica*, vol. 7, p. 1014; Bernard Martin, *A History of Judaism*, vol. II (New York: Basic Books, Inc. 1974) pp. 33, 168-171, 183-188.

50 "Belarus," *World Book Encyclopedia*, vol. 2, pp. 224 c-d; *Belarus, Then and Now*, M. Rodgers, T. Streissguth & C. Sexton, eds. (Minneapolis, MN: Lerner Publications Co., 1993), p. 43; Behrends, *The CIS*, p. 33.

51 *Belarus, Then and Now*, Rodgers, et. al., eds. p. 23.

52 Forty thousand Belarussians protested in mass outrage on April 26, 1996, the tenth anniversary of the Chernobyl disaster, according to Reuters, "Vigils Mark Nuclear Accident," *The Washington Post* (April 27, 1996): p. A20.

53 According to the Jewish Agency, the greatest increase in aliyah in 1996 from the CIS came from Belarus, and is attributed to the ghastly condition of the economy and political changes indicating the return of Communist methods of rule. Marilyn Henry, 'Against the trend," *The Jerusalem Post International Edition* (August 17, 1996): 21.

54 Hersch Smolar, *The Minsk Ghetto: Soviet-Jewish Partisans Against the Nazis* (New York: Holocaust Library, 1989), p. 88; "Minsk," *Encyclopedia of the Holocaust*, vol. 3 (New York: MacMillan Publishing Co., 1990), p. 975.

55 Smolar, *The Minsk Ghetto*, p. 73.

56 Felix's verbal account is supported in Smolar, *The Minsk Ghetto*, pp. 72-74, 88; "Minsk," *Encyclopedia Judaica*, vol. 12, pp. 54-55; see also Marilyn Henry, "The Bolt Out of Belarus," *The Jerusalem Post International Edition* (August 17, 1996):21.

57   Felix's verbal account is supported in Smolar, *The Minsk Ghetto*, pp. 98-101; "Minsk," *Encyclopedia Judaica*, vol. 12, p. 55; "Minsk," *Encyclopedia of the Holocaust*, vol. 3, p. 976.

58   Jews were herded into the Minsk Ghetto from areas of Germany, France, Poland, Czechoslovakia, Hungary and Greece. Smolar, *The Minsk Ghetto*, p. 98 (consistent with Felix's verbal account).

59   Felix' verbal account is supported in "Minsk," *Encyclopedia Judaica*, vol. 12, p. 56.

60   Felix's verbal account is supported in Smolar, *The Minsk Ghetto*, pp. 76-97; see also, "Minsk," *Encyclopedia Judaica*, vol. 12, pp. 55-56.

61   Faith in Jesus Christ did not exempt Jewish believers from extermination in the Holocaust. While the Nazis regarded these Messianic believers as Jewish, the mainstream Jewish community has not. It has not been possible to obtain an accurate estimate of how many Messianic Jews perished. Two Jewish believers' experiences during the Holocaust are recounted in Rachmiel Frydland, *When Being Jewish Was a Crime* (Nashville, TN: Thomas Nelson, Inc., 1978) and Jan Markell, *Trapped in Hitler's Hell* (Springfield, MO: Gospel Publishing House, 1985). See also, *The Voice of the Martyrs* (July 1995), p. 3.

62   Some of the Old Testament Scriptures supporting Gentile salvation include: Genesis 12:2-3; Psalms 67:2, 117, 86:9, 102:15-22; Isaiah 42:6, 49:6, 11:10, 2:2-3, 19:23-25, 14:1; Zephaniah 3:9; Amos 9:11-12; Ruth 1:16. These verses explicitly indicate the Gentiles are blessed and saved as Gentiles, not as "spiritual Israel" or "spiritual Jews."

63   See, for example, Isaiah 19:23-25, where God blesses the nations as distinct nations, not as part of ethnic Israel: "In that day there will be a highway from Egypt to Assyria. The Assyrians will go to Egypt and the Egyptians to Assyria. The Egyptians and Assyrians will worship together. In that day Israel will be the third, along with Egypt and Assyria, a blessing on the earth. The Lord Almighty will bless them, saying, 'Blessed be Egypt, My people, Assyria, My handiwork, and Israel, My inheritance.'"

[64] See, for example, Luke 24:46-47; Matthew 8:11-12; Luke 13:28-29; Matthew 24:14, 28:18-20.

[65] For a relatively recent discussion on the matter, see, for example, "The American Messianic Synagogue Movement: Deficiencies, Mistakes and Errors in Light of the Scriptures," a position paper issued in 1985 by the Elders Council of Grace Community Church in Los Angeles, California, and reprinted, together with Fruchtenbaum's response, in Fruchtenbaum, *Israelology*, pp. 917-949.

[66] For an overview of Messianic Judaism, see Fruchtenbaum, *Hebrew Christianity*; David Stern, *Messianic Jewish Manifesto* (Jerusalem, Israel: Jewish New Testament Publications, 1988); David Rausch, *Messianic Judaism: Its History, Theology and Polity* (New York: Edwin Mellen Press, 1982); Paul Liberman, *The Fig Tree Blossoms* (Indianola, IA: Fountain Press, 1989); Fruchtenbaum, *Israelology,* pp. 758-766, 857-949.

[67] Kai Kjaer-Hansen, *Joseph Rabinowitz and the Messianic Movement* (Grand Rapids, MI: Wm. B. Eerdmans Publishing Co.) 1995, pp. 67-74; Personal interview with Nellie Saganova, Committee of Religious Affairs, Kishinev, Moldova, August 1996.

[68] Kjaer-Hansen, *Joseph Rabinowitz*, p. 2.

[69] Personal interview with Nellie Saganova, Committee of Religious Affairs, Kishinev, Moldova, August 1996; Kjaer-Hansen, *Joseph Rabinowitz*, pp. 221-227.

[70] For a more thorough discussion, see Arthur F. Glasser, "Evangelical Objections to Jewish Evangelism," *Mishkan* 16:36-39 (1992).

[71] For a timely comment on Jewish evangelism, recognizing the Scriptural mandate to confront the Jews with the gospel in the context of respectful friendship, see Richard J. Mouw, "To the Jew First: Witnessing to the Jews is Non-Negotiable," *Christianity Today*, (August 11, 1997), p. 12.

72 See, for just one example, Semy Kahan, "Learning How to Prey," *The Jerusalem Post International Edition* (March 1, 1997): p. 15, which states the Christian Embassy in Jerusalem does not support Jewish missions—something Messianic Jews have known since the Embassy's inception.

73 See, for example, Timothy Morgan, "Jerusalem's Living Stones," *Christianity Today* (May 20, 1996), pp. 61-62; *Maoz* Newsletter (June 1996); Linda Alexander, *The Unpromised Land: The Story of Messianic Jews Gary and Shirley Beresford* (Baltimore, MD: Lederer Publications, 1994).

74 See, for example, Galatians 6:10; I Timothy 5:8; John 17:20-23, 21:15-17; I John 2:10, 3:14, 3:16-18, 3:23, 4:7, 4:11, 4:20-21; II John 5; III John 5; Matthew 25:31-46.

75 See, for example, Genesis 12:1-3; Psalms 67:1-2; Isaiah 42:6. 49:6; Galatians 3:8-9.

76 *Babi Yar: 1941-1991*, Simon Wiesenthal Center, ed. (Los Angeles, CA: Simon Wiesenthal Center, 1991), pp. 6-7, 11; Arnold and Silverstein, *Anti-Semitism: A Modern Perspective*, p. 91; Cang, *The Silent Millions*, p. 10; Rausch, *A Legacy of Hatred*, p. 120-121; "Babi Yar," *Encyclopedia of the Holocaust*, vol. 1, p. 133.

77 *Babi Yar*, Wiesenthal, ed. pp. 7, 13; Arnold and Silverstein, *Anti-Semitism: A Modern Perspective*, pp. 91-92; Cang, *The Silent Millions*, p. 11; Rausch, *A Legacy of Hatred*, p. 120-121; "Babi Yar," *Encyclopedia of the Holocaust*, vol. 1, p. 133.

78 *Babi Yar*, Wiesenthal, ed., pp. 13-15, 46; William Korey, "A Monument Over Babi Yar?" in *The Holocaust in the Soviet Union*, Lucjan Dobroszycki and Jefferey S. Gurock, eds., (Armonk, NY: M. E. Sharpe, Inc., 1993), p. 63; Arnold and Silverstein, *Anti-Semitism: A Modern Perspective*, p. 92; Cana, *The Silent Millions*, p. 11; Rausch, *A Legacy of Hatred*, p. 120.

79 *Babi Yar*, Wiesenthal, ed., p. 40; Rausch, *A Legacy of Hatred*, p.

120; Korey, "A Monument over Babi Yar?" in *The Holocaust in the Soviet Union*, Dobroszycki and Gurock, eds., p. 63.

[80] *Babi Yar*, Wiesenthal, ed., pp. 5, 9, 15; Arnold and Silverstein, *Anti-Semitism: A Modern Perspective*, p. 92; Cang, *The Silent Millions*, pp. 9, 11; Rausch, *A Legacy of Hatred*, p. 121; Flannery, *The Anguish of the Jews*, p. 238; Baron, *The Russian Jew*, p. 417; "Babi Yar," *Encyclopedia Judaica*, vol. 4, pp. 27-28; "Russia," *Encyclopedia Judaica*, vol. 14, pp. 475-476; "Babi Yar," *Encyclopedia of the Holocaust*, vol. 1, p. 134.

[81] *Babi Yar*, Wiesenthal, ed., pp. 7-8, 16-17; "Babi Yar," *Encyclopedia of the Holocaust*, vol. 1, pp. 134-135; "Babi Yar," *Encyclopedia Judaica*, vol. 4, p. 29.

[82] *Babi Yar*, Wiesenthal, ed., p. 12; Cang, *The Silent Millions*, p. 9; Rausch, *A Legacy of Hatred*, p. 120; Flannery, *The Anguish of the Jews*, p. 237; Baron, *The Russian Jew*, pp. 248-249; Zvi Gitelman, "Soviet Reactions to the Holocaust, 1945-1991," in *The Holocaust in the Soviet Union*, Dobroszycki and Gurock, eds., pp. 5-6.

[83] Gitelman, "Soviet Reactions to the Holocaust," in *The Holocaust in the Soviet Union*, Dobroszycki and Gurock, eds., p. 3.

[84] *Babi Yar*, Wiesenthal, ed., pp. 17-37; Korey, "A Monument Over Babi Yar?" in *The Holocaust in the Soviet Union*, Dobroszycki and Gurock, eds. pp. 64-74; Arnold and Silverstein, *Anti-Semitism: A Modern Perspective*, pp. 92-93; Cang, *The Silent Millions*, pp. 7-8, 12-13, 123-124; Flannery, *The Anguish of the Jews*, p. 238, Baron, *The Russian Jew*, pp. 416-417, n. 12; "Babi Yar," *Encyclopedia of the Holocaust*, vol. 1, p. 135; "Babi Yar," *Encyclopedia Judaica*, vol. 4, p. 30.

[85] Interestingly, it was recently reported that, on church grounds 150 miles from Kiev, two million Ukrainians have flocked to the site of a tree stump on which an image of a cross has appeared. Allegedly, many people have been miraculously healed by the cross. One local offered the following comment: "The communists used to execute people right here . . .

Hundreds of people have been shot here. There is too much evil around this place, too much blood." Associated Press, "Tree's symbol of life and death amazes believers in Ukraine," July 30, 1997.

[86] The State of Israel has officially recognized and honored as "Righteous Gentiles" those non-Jews who undertook special efforts during World War II to rescue Jews from Nazi hands. For additional information see, for example, Joseph J. Carr, *Christian Heroes of the Holocaust—The Righteous Gentiles* (South Plainfield, NJ: Bridge Publishing, Inc., 1984); Mordecai Paldiel, *The Path of the Righteous: Gentile Rescuers of Jews During the Holocaust* (Hoboken, NJ: KTAV Publishing House, Inc., 1993).

[87] As noted in Chapter 3, the Pale of Settlement was the region in czarist Russia to which the Jews were confined by law to live.

[88] V.D. Segre, "From Enlightenment to Socialism," in *The Zionist Movement in Palestine and World Politics, 1880-1918*, N. Gordon Levin, Jr., ed. (Lexington, MA: D.C. Heath and Co., 1974), p. 32; Walter Laqueur, *A History of Zionism* (New York: Schocken Books, 1976), pp. 75-77; Howard M. Sachar, *A History of Israel* (New York: Alfred A. Knopf, 1976), pp. 15-16; Baron, *The Russian Jew*, pp. 146-147; David Vital, *Zionism: The Formative Years* (Oxford: Clarendon Press, 1982), pp. 11-12.

[89] Sachar, *A History of Israel*, p. 16.

[90] David Vital, *The Origins of Zionism* (Oxford: Clarendon Press, 1980), pp. 179-180; see also, Kac, *Israel*, p. 76; "Russia," *Encyclopedia Judaica*, vol. 14, p. 444.

[91] Sachar, *A History of Israel*, pp. 16-17, 32; Baron, *The Russian Jew*, pp. 146-147; Vital, *The Origins of Zionism*, pp. 147-179; "Odessa Committee," *Encyclopedia Judaica*, vol. 12, pp. 1328-1329.

[92] Laqueur, *A History of Zionism*, p. 77.

[93] "Odessa," *Encyclopedia Judaica*, vol. 12, p. 1324.

[94] Ibid. Odessa also served as the point of exit for Christians throughout the Russian Empire making pilgrimage to the Holy Land. R. D. Kernohan, *The Road to Zion: Travelers to Palestine and the Land of Israel* (Grand Rapids, MI: Wm. B. Eerdmans Publishing Co., 1995), pp. 85-86, 90.

[95] Mark Wischnitzer, *To Dwell in Safety: The Story of Jewish Migration Since 1800* (Philadelphia, PA: The Jewish Publication Society of America, 1948), pp. 68, 86, 105-106, 112, 133; Ronald Sanders, *Shores of Refuge—A Hundred Years of Jewish Emigration* (New York: Henry Holt and Co., 1988), pp. 117, 122; Vital, *The Origins of Zionism*, p. 81; Laqueur, *A History of Zionism*, pp. 75, 563; *Encyclopedia of Zionism and Israel*, Raphael Patai, ed., vol. II (New York: Herzl Press/McGraw Hill, 1971), p. 984.

[96] Joan Comay, *Ben-Gurion and the Birth of Israel* (New York: Random House, 1967), p. 25.

[97] Declaration of Independence of the State of Israel (May 14, 1948), excerpt from Paragraph 4.

[98] "Messianic Movements," *Encyclopedia Judaica*, vol. 11, p. 1427; "Zionism," *Encyclopedia Judaica*, vol. 16, p. 1037; Kac, *Israel*, pp. 85-88; Arthur Hertzberg, *The Zionist Idea* (Westport, CT: Greenwood Press, 1959).

[99] Sachar, *A History of Israel*, pp. 15-17.

[100] Michael Pragai, *Faith and Fulfillment: Christians and the Return to the Promised Land* (London: Valentine, Mitchell, 1985), p. 4; Barbara Tuchman, *Bible and Sword: England and Palestine from the Bronze Age to Balfour* (New York: Ballantine Books, 1984), pp. 121-124, 177-192.

[101] "Zionism", *Encyclopedia Judaica*, vol. 16, p. 1153; David A. Rausch, *Fundamentalist Evangelicals and Anti-Semitism* (Valley Forge, PA:

Trinity Press International, 1993), pp. 19-29; David A. Rausch
, *Zionism Within Early American Fundamentalism 1878-1918*
(New York: The Edwin Mellen Press, 1979); Derek J. Tidball,
Who Are the Evangelicals? (London: HarperCollins Publishers,
1994), pp. 141-142; Malcolm Hedding, *Understanding Israel*
(Chicester, England: Sovereign World, Ltd., n.d.), pp. 10-14;
International Christian Embassy Jerusalem, *Christian Zionism
and its Biblical Basis* (Jerusalem: International Christian
Embassy Jerusalem, n.d.) pp. 9-12.

[102] See, for example, Pragai, *Faith and Fulfillment*, pp. 18-19.

[103] Genesis 13:15; 15:7; 17:7-8; 24:7; 26:2-3; 28:4, 13; 35:12; 48:4;
50:24; Deuteronomy 1:8; 6:10, 18; 7:8; 34:4; Psalms 105:8-11. Full
and continued possession of the land, however, has always been
contingent on Israel's obedience to God.

[104] Jeremiah 3:11-20; 12:14-17; 16:10-18; 23:1-8; 28:1-4; 29:1-14; 30:1-
3, 10-11; 31:2-14; 32:1-44; 42:1-22; 50:17-20; Ezekiel 20:39-44;
34:1-16; 35:1-37: 28; 39:21-29. In reference to the allotment of
land during the millennium, however, Ezekiel 47:21-22
interestingly instructs: "You are to distribute this land among
yourselves according to the tribes of Israel. You are to allot it as an
inheritance for yourselves and for the aliens who have settled
among you and who have children. You are to consider them as
native-born Israelites; along with you they are to be allotted an
inheritance among the tribes of Israel."

[105] See Fruchtenbaum, *Israelology*, pp. 634-636; Walvoord, *Israel in
Prophecy*, pp. 36-37, 65-66, 78-79; Walvoord, *Major Bible Prophecies*,
pp. 70-95; Robert L. Saucy, *The Case for Progressive
Dispensationalism: The Interface Between Dispensational and
Nondispensational Theology* (Grand Rapids, MI: Zondervan
Publishing House, 1993), pp. 50-57, 264-272.

[106] Pragai, *Faith and Fulfillment*, pp. 10-11: Tuchman, *Bible and Sword*,
p. 121; Franz Kobler, *The Vision Was There* (London: Lincolns-
Prager, Ltd., 1956), p. 13.

[107] Tuchman, *Bible and Sword*, p. 122; Kobler, *The Vision Was There*, p. 13.

[108] Tuchman, *Bible and Sword*, p. 121; Pragai, *Faith and Fulfillment*, p. 11.

[109] Tuchman, *Bible and Sword*, pp. 177, 182-183; Pragai, *Faith and Fulfillment*, p. 16.

[110] "Zionism," *Encyclopedia Judaica*, vol. 6, pp. 1153-1155; Kac, *Israel*, pp. 48-51; *A History of the Jewish People*, H. H. Ben-Sasson, ed. (Cambridge, MA: Harvard University Press, 1976), p. 893; Laqueur, *A History of Zionism*, p. 78.

[111] Tuchman, *Bible and Sword*, pp. 177-179; Pragai, *Faith and Fulfillment*, pp. 44-47; Kobler, *The Vision Was There*, pp. 59-65.

[112] Laurence Oliphant, *The Land of Gilead* (London: Wm. Blackwood and Sons, 1880), p. xxxiii-xxxv; Pragai, *Faith and Fulfillment*, pp. 53-55; Tuckman, *Bible and Sword*, pp. 270-272; Kobler, *The Vision Was There*, pp. 97-108.

[113] Kobler, *The Vision Was There*, p. 105.

[114] ICEJ, *Christian Zionism and Its Biblical Basis*, p. 11. For a more thorough discussion on Hechler's influence on Herzl, see, generally, Claude Duvernoy, *The Prince and the Prophet* (Christian Action for Israel, n.d.), transl. by Jack Joffe.

[115] Pragai, *Faith and Fulfillment*, p. 56.

[116] Wischnitzer, *To Dwell in Safety*, pp. 85-86; "Zionism," *Encyclopedia Judaica*, vol. 16, p. 1154; Kac, *Israel*, pp. 51-52; Pragai, *Faith and Fulfillment*, p. 57; Kobler, *The Vision Was There*, pp. 106-107.

[117] Kobler, *The Vision Was There*, p. 107.

[118] Franklyn Hudgings, *Zionism in Prophecy* (New York: Pro-Palestine Federation of America, 1936), pp. 27-29.

[119] "Zionism," *Encyclopedia Judaica*, vol. 16, p. 1155.

[120] See also Isaiah 14:2, 43:6

[121] Official census figures in 1995 estimated there to be 1.2 million Jews in the Former Soviet Union. However, for reasons stated in earlier chapters, that number can probably be doubled.

[122] Wischnitzer, *To Dwell in Safety*, p. 239.

[123] Yaacov Ro'i, *The Struggle for Soviet Jewish Emigration 1948-1967* (Cambridge, England: Cambridge University Press, 1991), p. 412.

[124] Ebenezer Emergency Fund, founded by Gustav Scheller, is headquartered in Bournemouth, U.K., with offices in Fort Collins, Colorado. See Jonathan Miles, "Christians help Bring Russian Jews to Israel," *Charisma* (April 1996), pp. 30-34; "Biblical Hunters Bringing Jews Out of Russia," *The Messianic Times* (July/August 1996), p. 31. Other Christian Zionist ministries, such as the International Christian Embassy Jerusalem, are also actively helping ex-Soviet Jews make aliyah.

[125] See, for example, Ezekiel 20:32-35, 22:17-22, 36:22-24, and Fruchtenbaum, *Israelology*, pp. 714-720. Some interpret Ezekiel 37:14 as also indicating a return to the land in unbelief.

[126] The biblical Year of Jubilee occurs every fifty years. It is a year of freedom and liberty, especially from debts and bondage. (Leviticus 25:10-13, et seq.)

[127] Ezekiel 29:16; Isaiah 30:1-3, 31:1; Jeremiah 42:13-18.

[128] *The Zondervan Pictorial Encyclopedia of the Bible*, Merrill C. Tenney, ed. (Grand Rapids, MI: Zondervan Publishing House, 1976), vol. 2, pp. 251-254.

[129] "Russia," *Encyclopedia Judaica*, vol. 14, p. 433; Baron, *The Russian Jew*, p. 2; Michael Davitt, *Within the Pale: The True*

Story of Anti-Semitic Persecution in Russia (New York: A. S. Barnes and Co., 1903), pp. 1-2.

130   Riasanovsky, *A History of Russia*, pp. 125, 394; Minton F. Goldman, *Commonwealth of Independent States and Central/Eastern Europe*, 4th ed. (Guilford, CT: Dushkin Publishing Group, Inc., 1992), pp. 5-6; Fedotov, *Russian Religious Mind*, pp. 397-400, 405; Benz, *Eastern Orthodox Church*, pp. 181-183; Nicolas Zernov, *The Russians and Their Church*, 3d ed. (Crestwood, NY: St. Vladimir's Press, 1978), pp. 47-49; Danzas, *The Russian Church*, pp. 26, 33-34, 106-107, 116-117.

131   Ezekiel 29:6, 9-12, 16; 30:8-9, 26; 32:15.

132   Veronica Ions, *Egyptian Mythology* (New York: Peter Bedrick Books, 1983), pp. 25, 36, 38-39; *Encyclopedia of Religion and Ethics*, James Hastings, ed. (New York: Charles Scribner's Sons, 1922) vol. 5, p. 245; *Encyclopedia Americana* (Danbury, CT: Grolier, Inc., 1993) vol. 7, p. 159.

133   *The NIV Study Bible, New International Version* (Grand Rapids, MI: Zondervan Publishing House, 1985), Study Note re: Exodus 14:2; *Baker Encyclopedia of the Bible*, Walter A. Elwell, ed. (Grand Rapids, MI: Baker Book House, 1988) vol. 1, p. 241.

134   See, for example, Kevin J. Conner, *Interpreting the Symbols and the Types*, rev. ed. (Portland, OR: Bible Temple Publishing, 1992), pp. 53-55, 157-158, 174; John J. Davis, *Biblical Numerology: A Basic Study of the Use of Numbers in the Bible* (Grand Rapids, MI: Baker Book House, 1968), pp. 122-123.

135   For more thorough discussion, see, generally, McCall and Levitt, *Coming: The End!*; Hitchcock, *After The Empire*.

136   *The New Scofield Reference Bible*, C. I. Scofield, ed. (New York: Oxford University Press, 1967), p. 881, n. 1; A. C. Gaebelein, *The Prophet Ezekiel: An Analytical Exposition* (New York: Our Hope, 1918) p.259; *The Bible Knowledge Commentary: Old Testament*, John F. Walvoord

and Roy B. Zuck, eds. (Wheaton, IL: Victor Books, 1985), pp. 1299-1300; H. A. Ironside, *Expository Notes on Ezekiel* (New York: Loizeaux Bros., Inc., 1949), pp. 266-267; John Walvoord, *Major Bible Prophecies*, pp. 328-330; McCall and Levitt, *Coming: The End!*, pp. 37-39; Hitchcock, *After The Empire*, pp. 13-39.

137 McCall and Levitt, *Coming: The End!*, p. 38; Hitchcock, *After The Empire*, pp. 18-19, 23: *Baker Encyclopedia of the Bible*, Elwell, ed., vol. 2, p. 1377; Ironside, *Ezekiel*, p. 266; Charles L. Feinberg, *The Prophecy of Ezekiel: The Glory of the Lord* (Chicago, IL: Moody Press, 1969), p.220; Helene Iswolsky, *Christ in Russia: The History, Tradition and Life of the Russian Church* (Milwaukee, WI: The Bruce Publishing Co., 1960), pp. 5-7.

138 McCall and Levitt, *Coming: The End!*, p. 39; Hitchcock, *After The Empire*, pp. 27, 55-57; Walvoord, *Major Bible Prophecies*, p. 330.

139 McCall and Levitt, *Coming: The End!*, pp. 38-39; Hitchcock, *After The Empire*, pp. 17-18. For alternative identification of the northern armies, see J. Paul Tanner, "Rethinking Ezekiel's Invasion by Gog," *Journal of the Evangelical Theological Society* (March 1996), vol. 39, no. 1, p. 29.

140 McCall and Levitt, *Coming: The End!*, pp. 101-128; Hitchcock, *After The Empire*, pp. 125-142. For alternative interpretations as to the timing of the invasion, see Feinberg, *Ezekiel*, pp. 218-219; *The Expositor's Bible Commentary*, Frank E. Gabelein, ed., vol. 6 (Grand Rapids, MI: Zondervan Publishing House, 1986), pp. 937-940.

141 David Hoffman, "Yeltsin Vows to 'Restore Order,' Pledges Government Shakeup," *The Washington Post* (March 7, 1997): p. A1.

142 See, for example, David Hoffman, "Goods Replace Rubles in Russia's Vast Web of Trade," *The Washington Post* (January 31, 1997): pp. A15, 17; Hoffman, "Despite Yeltsin's Promises, Workers Remain Unpaid," *The Washington Post* (March 16, 1997): p. A24; Hoffman, "Yeltsin's Foes Blocked in Bid to Unseat Him," *The Washington Post* (January 23, 1997): pp. A19, 21.

[143] Lee Hockstader, "Lebed in Waiting," *The Washington Post* (January 14, 1997): p. A9; David Hoffman, "Lebed Firing Sets Stage for Long Battle," *The Washington Post* (October 18, 1996): pp. A41, 44.

[144] Lee Hockstader, "Yeltsin Adviser Blasts Foreign Cultures, Sects," *The Washington Post* (June 28, 1996): p. A23; Nickels, "Growing Nationalism," *Christianity Today* (August 12, 1996): p. 54.

[145] Statement by Alexei Mitrofanov, as quoted in Michael Kramer, "The People Choose," *Time* (May 27, 1996), p. 53; see also, Lee Hockstader, "Zyuganov Heads Anti-Yeltsin Alliance," *The Washington Post* (August 8, 1996): p. A26.

[146] See, for example, David Hoffman, "Zyuganov Praises Stalin, Blames West for Soviet Collapse," *The Washington Post* (May 13, 1996): p. A12; Lee Hockstader, "Russian Orthodox Church is Feeling Rebirth Pains: Critics Accuse It of Coziness with Government," *The Washington Post* (April 14, 1996): p. A16; David Hoffman, "Russia Closing More Offices of Jewish Emigration Agency," *The Washington Post* (June 12, 1996): p. A26; Reuters, "Zhirinovsky Hails Buchanan, Says Could Deport Jews," (February 22, 1996); James Carney, "A Communist to His Roots," *Time* (May 27, 1996), pp. 61-62; Hitchcock, *After The Empire*, pp. 46-54; G. A. Zyuganov, *Za Gorizontom* (Moscow, Russia: Informpechat, 1995), pp. 17-18.

[147] See, for example, Lee Hockstader, "New Russian Communists Put on a Moderate Face," *The Washington Post* (May 20, 1996): pp. A1, 16.

[148] The Union of Councils for Soviet Jews, founded in 1970, is headquartered in Washington, DC. The UCSJ works with indigenous human rights and Jewish activist groups to promote human rights generally, and the security, freedom and welfare of Jews in the Former Soviet Union.

[149] Beverly Nickles, "Will Growing Nationalism Stall Christian Outreach?," *Christianity Today* (August 12, 1996): p. 54; *National and International Religion Report*, vol. 10, no. 13 (June 24, 1996), pp. 7-8.

[150] *National and International Religion Report*, vol. 10, no. 13 (June 24, 1996), pp. 7-8; Beverly Nickles, "Will Growing Nationalism Stall Christian Outreach?" *Christianity Today* (August 12, 1996): p. 54.

[151] David Hoffman, "Russia Passes Bill Curbing Some Faiths," *The Washington Post* (September 25, 1997), p. A1; Maura Reynolds, "Yeltsin Signs Religion Bill," Associated Press, September 26, 1997; see also Beverly Nickles, "Religious Freedom Faces Cutback," *Christianity Today* (August 11, 1997), p. 61.

[152] Associated Press, "Details of Russia Religion Law," September 26, 1997.

[153] Beverly Nickles, "New Religion Law Fraught with Potential for Abuse," *Christianity Today* (November 17, 1997), p. 66.

[153] Maura Reynolds, "Yeltsin Signs Religion Bill," Associated Press, September 26, 1997.

[154] Among other news reports from foreign missions, see, for example, Slavic Gospel Association, *Insight* (April 1997): pp. 3-4.

[155] Associated Press, "U.S. Aid to Belarus Suspended," *The Washington Post* (March 22, 1997), p. A19; Lee Hockstader, "Belarus Detains U.S. Diplomat Monitoring Protest, Plans to Expel Him," *The Washington Post* (March 24, 1997): p. A14.

[156] Marina Babkina, Associated Press, "Russia, Belarus Ties at Impasse," August 21, 1997; "Foundation says it was forced out of Belarus," *The Orange County Register* (September 4, 1997) , p. 20.

[157] Slavic Gospel Association, "Belarus Protests Continue to Escalate," *Insight* (May 1997), p. 3.

[158] Union of Councils for Soviet Jews, *Anti-Semitism in the Former Soviet Union—Report—1995-1997*, (Washington, DC) , 1997, pp. 155-166.

[159] Michael Dobbs, "Political Shift in Belarus Poses U.S. Policy Dilemma," *The Washington Post* (April 4, 1997): p. A17.

[160] Lee Hockstader, "Belarus, Russia Move Toward a New Union," *The Washington Post* (April 3, 1997): pp. A23, 28.

[161] Barton Gellman, "Russia Bars Activity by Israeli Panel," *The Washington Post* (May 1, 1996): p. A21; Batsheva Tsur and Marilyn Henry, "U.S. Concerned After Russia Closes Two Jewish Agency Centers," *The Jerusalem Post International Edition* (May 11, 1996): p. 3.

[162] Marilyn Henry and Batsheva Tsur, "Agency 'Interfering' in Russian Affairs," *The Jerusalem Post International Edition* (May 25, 1996): p. 3; Steve Rodan, "To Russia with Doubts," *The Jerusalem Post International Edition* (March 1, 1997): p. 18.

[163] Hoffman, "Russia Closing More Offices," *The Washington Post* (June 12, 1996), pp. A1, 26. See also, "Fire Destroys Moscow Synagogue," *The Jerusalem Post International Edition* (July 27, 1996), p. 6.

[164] Jerusalem Post Staff, "Yeltsin: Russia Will Not Arm Syria," *The Jerusalem Post International Edition* (March 22, 1997): p. 32; Associated Press, "Netanyahu Advises Russia on Iran" (February 22, 1998).

[165] Hoffman, "Russia Bars Activity," *The Washington Post* (May 1, 1996): p. A21; Tsur and Henry, "US Concerned," *The Jerusalem Post International Edition* (May 11, 1996): p. 3; David Makovsky, "Former Soviet Property in Jerusalem Transferred to Russia," *The Jerusalem Post International Edition* (May 4, 1996): p. 3; David Hoffman, "Yeltsin, Rival Differ on Ties to the West," *The Washington Post* (May 30, 1996): p. A28; Dimitri K. Simes, "Russia: Still a Bear," *The Washington Post* (July 9, 1996), p. A15; Jerusalem Post Staff, "Yeltsin: Russia Will Not Arm Syria," *The Jerusalem Post International Edition* (March 22, 1997): p. 32.

[166] The fact the Jews have been given custody of the Land does not mean they have been given license to mistreat foreigners dwelling there.

[167] See, for example, Soviet Prisoners of Zion, "An Appeal to the Government of Israel," *The Jerusalem Post International Edition*

(March 9, 1996): p. 11; Daniel Williams, "Ex-Soviet Jews' Shift to Right Hurts Peres—Immigrant Bloc in Israel is Skeptical of Peace Moves," *The Washington Post* (May 22, 1996): pp. A23-24.

[168] See, for example, *National and International Religion Report*, vol. 10, no. 13 (June 14, 1996), p. 8.

[169] Ben Levinson, "Israel Considers Anti-Missionary Law," *Charisma* (August 1997): p. 20.

[170] Haim Shapiro, "WJC warns of missionary activity," *The Jerusalem Post International Edition* (August 3, 1996): p. 32.

[171] S. Aaron Osborne, "Christians Protest Proposed Anti-Missionary Legislation," *Christianity Today* (May 19, 1997) vol. 41, no. 6, p. 55.

[172] Ben Levinson, "Israel Considers Anti-Missionary Law," *Charisma* (August 1997): p. 20.

[173] Hillel Kuttler, "US Christians Protest Bill Limiting Missionary Activity in Israel," *The Jerusalem Post International Edition* (June 7, 1997): p. 4. Osborne, "Christians Protest," *Christianity Today* (May 19, 1997) vol. 41, no. 6, p. 55; *Maoz* Newsletter (June 1997), pp. 5-6.

[174] A book providing valuable insight on how to pray for Israel and the Jewish people, is Reuven Doron, *One New Man* (Cedar Rapids, IA: Embrace, 1993).

[175] Exact numbers are hard to obtain, partly because many believers are, in effect, underground, but see Morgan, "Living Stones," *Christianity Today* (May 20, 1996), pp. 62-63; David Dolan, "A Special Moment for Israel," *Charisma* (April 1995), p. 20.

[176] See, for example, "Partying with the Russians," *The Jerusalem Post International Edition* (April 27, 1996), p. 22; Williams, "Ex-Soviet Jews' Shift," *The Washington Post* (May 22, 1996), pp. A23-24; M. K. Guzda, "Little Parties Suddenly Loom Large in Israel," *The Washington Post* (May 31, 1996), p. A 28.

177 See, for example, Morgan, "Living Stones," *Christianity Today* (May 20, 1996), pp. 61-62.

178 See, for example, Beverly Nickles, "Training Shortfall May Imperil Growth," *Christianity Today* (April 7, 1997): p. 54.

179 F. F. Bruce, *The Epistle of Paul to the Romans* in *The Tyndale New Testament Commentaries*, R.V.G. Tasker, ed. (Grand Rapids, MI: Wm. B. Eerdmans Publishing Co., 1963), pp. 217-218.

180 "All Israel" is understood by theologians in different ways. The most biblically sound interpretation is that the overwhelming majority, including Israel's leaders who are alive at the time, will be saved when God pours out His Spirit on the Jews. It does not mean that all Jews who ever lived will be saved. See, for example, Fruchtenbaum, *Israelology*, p. 785; Bruce, *Romans*, in *Commentaries*, Tasker, ed., pp. 221-222.

181 Prophecies not already discussed in this book include: Genesis 3:15, 12:3, 18:18, 49:10; Deuteronomy 18:15, 19; Psalms 2:7, 16:10, 22, 41:9, 68:18, 69:21, 110:1, 118:22-23, 132:11; Isaiah 7:14*, 9:1-8, 11:10, 42:1-3, 49:1-8, 50:6, 52:13-53:12*, 59:16, 61:1-11; Jeremiah 23:5-6*, 31:31-33*, 33:15; Daniel 9:24-26* (predicts the time of Messiah's coming); Micah 5:2.*

* Denotes especially significant Messianic prophecies.